Going Through the Mystery's One Hundred Questions

Tongxuan Baiwen 通玄百問 第1卷

Yuxi Tongxuan Temple, Great Meditation Teacher
Yuantong raised the questions; Mahabodhi Monastery,
Venerable Wansong respectfully answered;
the old man, Longyan Linquan [wrote] verses;
person of the way Shengshen of Huating [donated]
printing blocks.

Dosho Port

Going Through the Mystery's One Hundred Questions
Dosho Port

Published by
The Sumeru Press Inc.
PO Box 75, Manotick Main Post Office,
Manotick, ON, Canada K4M 1A2

ISBN 978-1-896559-88-9

LIBRARY AND ARCHIVES CANADA CATALOGUING IN PUBLICATION

Title: Going through the mystery's one hundred questions / Dosho Port.
Names: Port, Dosho, author.
Description: "Yuxi Tongxuan Temple, Great Meditation Teacher
    Yuantong raised the questions;
Mahabodhi Monastery, Venerable Wansong respectfully answered; the
    old man, Longyan Linquan [wrote] verses;
person of the way Shengshen of Huating [donated] printing blocks." |
    Includes bibliographical references. | Text in English; some text in
    Chinese.
Identifiers: Canadiana 20220412367 | ISBN 9781896559889
    (softcover)
Subjects: LCSH: Spiritual life—Zen Buddhism—Miscellanea. | LCSH:
    Zen Buddhism—China.
Classification: LCC BQ9289 .P67 2022 | DDC 294.3/9270951—dc23

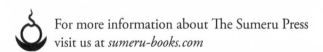

For more information about The Sumeru Press
visit us at *sumeru-books.com*

"I wish to have living beings
Eliminate doubts, abandon wrongly held views,
And give rise to correct Mahayana faith,
Leaving the buddha-lineage unbroken."[1]

Ashvagosha *(Neighing Horses)*

---

1   *Treatise on Awakening Mahayana Faith*, Edited and translated by John Jorgensen,
Dan Lusthaus, John Makeham and Mark Strange. Modified.

Contents

Acknowledgements

First, I want to thank my best friend and best wife ever, my co-teacher with Vine of Obstacles Zen, Tetsugan Zummach Sensei. Without her, I have no idea where I'd be and what I'd be doing, but I'm confident that I would not be publishing my third dharma book. She inspires me with clear wisdom and tender yet fierce compassion every day. So a whole-hearted "Thank you!" goes out to her.

Second, I've been so gifted in this life with teachers of the formal kind, starting in 1977 with Dainin Katagiri Roshi. Harada Tangen Roshi and the monks at Bukkokuji showed me a way of practicing-awakening that I hadn't yet dreamed was possible. Daido Loori Roshi sat with me after sesshin and smoked cigars. Good cigars and really good Zen talk. Melissa Myozen Blacker Roshi and David Dae An Rynick Roshi worked through many old cases with me, as did James Myoun Ford Roshi, who gave me inka shomei (印可証明) after thirty-five years of training in this Zen Way. I bow to you all every day.[1]

Third, I thank the students of the Vine of Obstacles Zen, past, present, and future, for their wholehearted exploration of the dharma and their generosity while walking this Zen way together.

Fourth, Kokyo Henkel Sensei reviewed the manuscript and made many valuable suggestions. His broad and in-depth knowledge of the buddhadharma is an inspiration to me.

Fifth, thanks to David Shujo Pettersen for creating the Select Lines in the Caodong Lineage table that appears at the end of the Introduction and then futzing with it until it was just right.

Finally, I thank my parents, Bob and Jean Port, who started going steady seventy-three years ago and are still joking about who asked whom and whether it was a good idea or not. In my view, of course, it was a very good idea. After more than forty-five years away, it is such a pleasure to live near them again and share some more laughs.

---

1   Inka shomei, literally "seal certified, clearly proven" is the final step in the process of authorization of a Zen teacher.

Introduction

Why?

Why study this or any Buddhist text?

Primarily, within buddhadharma, we study to realize the same mind as the Buddha so that we can embody Buddha through the twenty-four hours. In this light, along with zazen and engagement in the world, study is one of the three key aspects of Zen practice.

Why this text?

In *Going Through the Mystery's One Hundred Questions*, we sit together with a passionate Zen pilgrim, Yuantong (圓通, n.d.), and his cold-blooded teacher, the Caodong lineage master Wansong Xingxiu (萬松行秀, 1166-1246, Japanese, Bansho Gyoshu).[2] They hail to us from sometime in the 1220's, near the end of the classic period of Zen in China. We get to listen as a sincere student asks burning, heartfelt question after question. And an authentic teacher responds with turning word after turning word. We are able to eavesdrop on their teacher-student relationship due to the presence of Wansong's sterling attendant, Linquan Conglun (林泉從倫, n.d., Japanese, Rinsen Jurin), who also became a famous Zen master. Incredible!

In Linquan's verse for "Question 67: Where is the treasure land?", he describes for us the process of Zen practice:

> The pearl in your clothes is clearly obvious
> Just the tinkling of jewelry as you stagger along
> cleansed by being blown about in the whirlwind

We are already fully endowed with the radiant light of Buddha – the pearl is sewn into the very clothes we are wearing now. And in our efforts, while we're staggering along together to realize the same mind as Buddha, the tinkling of the jewelry is clear and present from our first efforts, through to and including great awakening and post-awakening training. The whirlwind of this world of dew, the process itself, is thoroughly purifying.

Yuantong models this process for us in each of his one hundred questions.

---

2   Japanese pronunciation of the Chinese characters will be given when the person is
     widely known by that pronunciation, for example, in the case of those monks in
     the Caodong lineage that led to Dogen and modern Soto Zen.

Plunging into the Depths of Zen

What does Yuantong ask?

Yuantong aspires to great awakening and is looking for some help. He sometimes seems to think that clear intellectual understanding is what he's lacking. At other times, he seems to get that there is something that he doesn't get, and can't get with his usual way of understanding, and yet is at a loss for what else to do. For those of you who are seekers, I expect that this will feel quite familiar.

About half of Yuantong's questions directly reference a koan or a sutra, revealing a deep and subtle fluency with the buddhadharma, and a propensity for the Koan Way. The other half are questions for which I've found neither koan nor sutra references. These questions come from the unadorned heart of this earnest seeker for the wisdom life of the Buddhas. However, this group of questions may not be as large as it seems, because I'm sure I've missed some of the references.

Wansong's responses to Yuantong often come with a twinkling sense of humor and reveal his great patience with Yuantong's process. Wansong presents the view of a deeply realized master and waits for Yuantong to exhaust his proclivity to look away. Wansong's answers are only a few characters in length – unlike most Zen teachers these days, myself included, who have a propensity to pontificate.

Linquan, the attendant who took notes from these questions and answers, also wrote verses for each interaction later on, notably free from any character or rhyming pattern. Except that almost every verse begins with Wansong's response and then explodes.

This text, then, includes one hundred questions, one hundred answers, and one hundred verses. In addition, I've added chapter titles and one hundred commentaries to help you, the contemporary reader, explore the inner points of the dialogues. If you carefully, slowly, intimately steep your bodymind in this text, reading from the belly, peeking out through your navel – rather than your frontal lobe – you will see what it's like for the buddhadharma to be thoroughly digested, so that it is expressed in the simplest of forms. If you engage in such exploration, you'll find yourself plunging into the depths of Zen.

You will, however, notice almost no trace of the Caodong lineage as something distinct from other lines of the Zen Way, particularly, the Linji Way. In fact, if we can judge from Yuantong raising more questions involving koans from Linji masters than from Caodong masters, he seems somewhat more interested in understanding teachings from the Linji lineage than from the Caodong line.

As we go forward into the next sections of the Introduction, I will share more biographical background on Wansong and Linquan. We'll meet earnest Way seekers concerned about the awakened truth of the buddhadharma, and enjoying the opportunity to walk along the ancient road together, warm hand to warm hand. You yourself might stretch out a hand too, and find yourself strolling along with Wansong, Linquan, and Yuantong.

Who was this seeker, Yuantong? Beyond what's recorded here in *Going Through the Mystery's One Hundred Questions*, little is known. His name, Yuantong (圓通) means "Perfectly Penetrating," and Linquan refers to him above as "Great Teacher" (大禪). Linquan also notes that he was from the city of Yuxi and resided at Going Through the Mystery Hermitage (通玄庵), and thus the name of the text. Yuantong may have been a meditation master at the time of inquiring of Wansong, however his dharma candle had not yet been lit. Happily, though, as we'll see below, Linquan tells us that he did realize great awakening sometime after he'd asked his one hundred questions.

Much more is known about Wansong and Linquan, so let's now spend some time with each of them in turn.

Wansong Xingxiu and the Caodong Lineage

Now I want to tell you about Wansong's great dharma journey, focusing my narrative lens on his awakening experiences. Get ready for some intense koan and dharma genealogy. Because everything arises in context and is inseparable from context, there's going to be a good deal of that in the coming pages. My advice: keep a keen eye out for what's most important by noticing your own psychophysical changes. Specifically: What gives energy for the Way? What depletes energy for the Way?

Those of you who are interested in the details of the genealogy are invited to spend some time with the table, Select Lines from the Caodong Lineage, that appears at the end of this introduction. Those of you who want to spend some time with the twists and turns of the koans are encouraged to do so as well, of course, and please know that to plumb the depths of the Koan Way, you will need to find a good teacher authorized to teach it who also presently has a pulse.

As I said, I want to tell you about Wansong's dharma journey, so here we go. He was born in what is now Yuncheng, about 600 miles southeast of Beijing. At fifteen, Wansong traveled 300 miles northeast to what is now the city of Xingtai and became a monk, receiving the ordination name Xingxiu (行秀, Excellent Practice). The name "Wansong" comes later, so hold on.

After full ordination, probably when he turned eighteen, he traveled 1100 miles back to the southeast to Qingshousi, a hotspot on the Silk Road, to study with Shengmo Guang (勝默光, n.d.), a fifth generation successor of the important revitalizer of the Caodong lineage, Furong Daokai (芙蓉道楷, 1043-1118, Japanese, Fuyo Dokai).

Daokai was an 18th generation Chinese ancestor of the great Indian sage, Bodhidharma. From our contemporary perspective, Daokai's two most important successors were Danxia Zichun (丹霞子淳, 1064-1119, Japanese, Tanka Shijun) and Lumen Zijue (鹿門自覺, d.1117, Japanese, Rokumon Jikaku). Zichun's successors would include Hongzhi Zhengjue (宏智正覺, 1091-1157, Japanese, Wanshi Shogaku) and in the fifth generation through Zhenxie Qingliao (真歇清了, 1090-1151, Japanese, Choro Seiryo), the Japanese monk, Eihei Dogen (永平道元, 1200-1253). Shengmo's teacher was Yushan Shiti (玉山師體, n.d.), fourth generation from Daokai in the Lumen line.

The Dharma Mirror of the Ancestors, Scroll 70, has this about Wansong's first awakening:

> At first, Wansong practiced with Venerable Shengmo, examining Changsha's words, "Turn oneself around in the mountains, rivers, and the great earth." After six months, Shengmo said, "I only wish you a late realization." Wansong suddenly had insight.[3]

It is notable that the Caodong master Shengmo assigned the young Wansong a key phrase from a koan, Changsha's words, "Turn oneself around in the mountains, rivers, and the great earth," a practice that is more associated nowadays with the Linji/Rinzai lineage. The contemporary narrative about the Caodong in this period is that the main practice was silent illumination (默照, mozhao). However, there is no support for this in *Going Through the Mystery's One Hundred Questions*. The closest the text comes to mentioning silent illumination is in "Question 9: How is thusness meditation practiced?" However, thusness meditation is based on *The Lankavatara Sutra*, a favorite of Bodhidharma, and so it is a query that might well be common to all Zen lineages.

Let's return now to Wansong's story.

After just six months of work on the koan "Changsha's Mountains, Rivers, and the Great Earth," it is striking that Shengmo would only wish the young Wansong an awakening *later* in life. How about right now? I hear Shengmo saying, "Really steep yourself deeply in buddhadharma, and don't worry about forced intimations of the great truth."

This is much like Shengmo's Linji lineage contemporary, Yunan (運庵, 1156-1226, Japanese, Un'an Fugan), advising Xutang (虛堂, 1185-1269, Japanese, Kido), who was also struggling with a breakthrough

---

3   *The Dharma Mirror of the Ancestors*, Scroll 70, https://amp.blog.shops-net. com/47079767/1/wansong-xingxiu.html, trans., Dosho Port (unpublished).

koan, "Take it easy, just remain mindless and unfettered by words."[4]

It must have been an unexpected relief for Wansong to hear Shengmo wish him realization sometime later, so much so that Wansong immediately had an insight. Although Wansong did not stay long with Shengmo, the impact of his first teacher was long lasting. In his best-known work, *The Record of Going Easy*, he cites Shengmo four times, including this in "Case 47: Zhaozhou's Oak Tree:"

> Venerable Shengmo had people pass through this case first, cleansing prior knowledge. He once said, "The three mysteries[5] and the five ranks are entirely in this."[6]

Again, we have the Caodong lineage master, Shengmo, usually assigning Zhouzhao's Oak Tree as the first koan, suggesting that there were more cases to follow, maybe a mini curriculum, possibly idiosyncratic to Shengmo, including the koan assigned to Wansong. Additionally, Shengmo speaks the language of the One Zen School by including the Three Mysteries, a teaching system first used in the Linji line, and the Five Ranks, a teaching device of Dongshan Liangjie (洞山良价, 807-869) in what became known as the Caodong line. However, Dongshan's five ranks in our day are primarily taken up by students in Rinzai Zen or by Soto (or Sanbo) Zen students doing koan introspection within the Harada-Yasutani koan curriculum.

Soon after his initial breakthrough, for reasons not given, Wansong traveled about 1000 miles back to the northeast to Cizhou to study with Xueyan Huiman (雪巖慧滿, d. 1206), also a successor of Yushan Shiti, like Shengmo. Keep in mind that a 1000 mile walk in straw sandals at the brisk clip of twenty miles a day would take the better part of two months. If all went well.

Let's enter Xueyan's inner room with Wansong:

Then Wansong examined Xuansha's words, "Not yet

---

4   Hakuin Zenji, *Complete Poison Blossoms from a Thicket of Thorn: The Zen Records of Hakuin Zenji*, trans., Norman Waddell (Berkeley, CA: Counterpoint, 2017), 344-45.

5   Linji's Three Mysteries are mysterious, but Kirscher has this: (1) its absolute state, (2) its manifestations as intrinsic wisdom and the functioning of this wisdom, and (3) its manifestation through humans and their activities. We may speak of the Three Statements, the Three Essential States, and the Three Mysteries, but these are all mutually related and in the end are but a way of observing the one reality. See *The Record of Linji*, trans., Ruth Fuller Sasaki, edit. Thomas Yuho Kirchner (Honolulu: University of Hawai'i Press, 2009), 144-145.

6   Wansong Xingxiu, *The Record of Going Easy*, Case 47: Zhaozhou 's Oak Tree, trans., Dosho Port (unpublished).

thoroughly realized." Xueyan said, "You wait for a horn to grow from your head, until your hands and feet grow teeth and claws." Then Xueyan struck with his staff. Later, Wansong happened to see a flying rooster crowing and greatly awakened. He said, "Today I not only seized Xuansha's old tiger. I also seized Changsha Jingcen's great tiger." Xueyan said, "In that case, I laugh with you. You were born with teeth and claws, but their sharp points were not revealed. Mountains and rivers revolve, yet every inch hits the mark. You have the special spirit of a lone rhinoceros passing through."[7]

Wansong had already had an initial breakthrough, and now under Xueyan's guidance, he took up a phrase attributed to Xuansha, with no small amount of irony, "Not yet thoroughly realized." Then Xueyan gave him an encouraging scolding for awaiting awakening. Earlier, Shengmo had only wished for him to come to enlightenment late in life.

The contrast must have made the young Wansong's head spin. Soon after Xueyan's rebuke, Wansong heard the crow of a flying rooster and was startled into sudden great awakening. His first post-awakening utterance, "Today I not only seized Xuansha's old tiger, I also seized Changsha Jingcen's great tiger," probably refers primarily to the two koans that he had passed through. Secondarily, Changsha Jingcen is also known as Cen the Tiger due to this encounter with Yangshan:

> One evening Changsha Jingcen was enjoying the moon. Yangshan Huiji pointed to it and said, "Everyone without exception has that. They're just unable to use it." Changsha replied, "Precisely. So let's see you use it." Yangshan said, "You try using it!" Thereupon Changsha gave Yangshan a kick and knocked him down. Getting up, Yangshan said, "Teacher, you're just like a tiger."[8]

Just like a tiger. Just like the crow of a flying rooster.

Xueyan's confirmation includes references to his earlier rebuke, "You were born with teeth and claws, but their sharp points were not revealed," and Wansong's first koan, "Mountains and rivers revolve, yet every inch hits the mark."

The great perfection made manifest, Xueyan caps his verification with

---

7   *Dharma Mirror of the Ancestors*, Scroll 70, https://amp.blog.shops-net.com/47079767/1/wansong-xingxiu.html, trans., Dosho Port (unpublished).

8   *Entangling Vines: A Classic Collection of Zen Koans*, trans., Thomas Yuho Kirchner (Somerville, MA: Wisdom, 2013), 171.

"You have the special spirit of a lone rhinoceros passing through." He may have had *The Khaggavisana Sutta* in mind, a sutta in the Pali Canon composed of forty verses, thirty-eight that compare a noble practitioner to a lone rhinoceros passing through. Here's one such verse:

> Transcending the contortion of views,
> the sure way attained,
> the path gained,
> "Unled by others,
> I have knowledge arisen,"
> wander alone
> like a rhinoceros.[9]

After his awakening and confirmation, Wansong wrote the following verse, "The Seal of Profound Accord:"

> At midnight a golden rooster took off crowing
> It's not enough to rouse a secluded person from a dream
> Clouds break up as the moon, the stars, and Big Dipper
> quake
> Seize the great tiger, the eye of unhindered freedom[10]

In Chinese mythology, the rooster's goldenness is due to its capacity to wake people from sleep. Here the rooster's crow profoundly awakened Wansong from ignorance, shaking the sun, moon, and stars.

Wansong stayed with Xueyan for two years, continuing to clarify his eye of unhindered freedom. He then retreated to a hermitage for sacred-womb training in an area called Ten Thousand Pines (Chinese, Wansong). It is here that he would take on the name "Old Man of Ten Thousand Pines" (Wansong Laoren 萬松老人).

Wansong seems to have spent only a few years in hermit practice. He would have been in his late twenties when, in 1193, the Jin emperor of the breakaway region of northern China invited him to the capital, present-day Beijing. So "Old" could not be a reference to Wansong's physical age but must refer to timelessness. "Old" like a lone rhinoceros. "Old" like Shakyamuni, "In heaven and on earth, I alone am the honored one."

---

9   *Khaggavisana Sutta: A Rhinoceros*, trans., Thanissaro Bhikkhu, https://www. accesstoinsight.org/tipitaka/kn/snp/snp.1.03.than.html.

10 *Dharma Mirror of the Ancestors*, Scroll 70, https://amp.blog.shops-net. com/47079767/1/wansong-xingxiu.html, trans., Dosho Port (unpublished). This verse could also have been written by Xueyan to confirm Wansong's awakening. The text is not clear.

Young or old, the Jin emperor gave the Old Man a brocade robe, and after a few years installed him as abbot of Bao'en Monastery (寶恩寺). Wansong lived in the Congrong Hermitage (從容庵), where he remained even through the Mongol sacking of the capitol in 1215.

In 1223, Yelu Chucai sought his instruction.

> One of Wansong's main lay followers was the well-educated and philosophically astute Khitan diplomat Yelu Chucai (1190-1243), an important advisor to Genghis and his son, Ogodei. Yelu helped convince Wansong that there needed to be an outstanding published record of his teachings in order for Caodong Chan to compete with various rivals, especially Tibetan Buddhism in addition to other movements including Daoism and the increasingly influential Christianity.[11]

From this prompting, Wansong's *The Record of Going Easy* was born. Steven Heine summarizes the contents as follows:

> The text as derived from the verse remarks (songgu) on one hundred cases originally created by another eminent leader of the Caodong school, Hongzhi Zhenjue (1091-1157), follows almost exactly *The Blue Cliff Record*'s formula of containing seven sections for each case: an (1) introduction, the (2) gongan selected by Hongzhi with (3) Wansong's capping phrases followed by his (4) prose comments, and (5) Hongzhi's verse with (6) Wansong's capping phrases followed by (7) prose remarks.[12]

Heine further reports that "According to some accounts an early manuscript was lost, but in 1224, Wansong's masterpiece was published and soon after was widely distributed in the northern territory while also gaining the attention of Mongol rulers."

The Record of Going Easy remains an important text today, particularly in Japanese Soto Zen and for Western koan students working in the Harada-Yasutani in-the-room koan introspection.

Wansong also wrote capping phrases and commentary for another koan collection with cases and verses gathered and authored by Hongzhi, *Record of Getting to the Point*. As for the present work, *Going Through the Mystery's One Hundred Questions*, I turn again to the inimitable Steven

---

11 Steven Heine, *Chan Rhetoric of Uncertainty in the Blue Cliff Record: Sharpening a Sword at the Dragon Gate* (New York: Oxford University Press, 2016), 229.

12 Ibid.

Heine for a short summary:

> Wansong also published two additional texts, Tongxuan's
> *[Going Through the Mystery's] One Hundred Questions* 通
> 玄百問 *(Tongxuan Baiwen)* and *Qingzhou's One Hun-*
> *dred Questions* 青州百問 *(Qingzhou Baiwen)*, in which
> a monk asks a series of questions to which Wansong
> gives concise and cryptic gongan-like responses. Both
> collections were first published in the 1240's, but some-
> time later Wansong's equally prolific disciple Linquan
> added verse comments for each question and answer.[13]

In 1230, Wansong continued teaching through the patronage of the Mongol rulers and became abbot of Wanshou Monastery (萬壽寺, Ten Thousand Lifetimes Monastery), also in what is now known as Beijing. He left
Linquan as his successor at Bao'en Monastery. According to Linquan's
preface for *Going Through the Mystery's One Hundred Questions*, shared in
full below, Yuantong was another of Wansong's successors, the second of
four that I've located.

The third successor of Wansong was Xueting Fuyu (雪庭福裕, 1203-
1275). According to Jiang Wu,

> One of [Wansong's] disciples, Xueting Fuyu, was ap-
> pointed abbot of the famed Shaolin monastery and
> greatly promoted the Caodong school. Since then, de-
> spite the decline of Buddhism during the early- and mid-
> Ming, the Caodong transmission in Shaolin monastery is
> believed to have been maintained without disruption."[14]

In this whirlwind world of constant flow, this is a remarkable and perhaps
unmatched record of lineage succession of a major monastery, the monastery just down the mountain from where the great Bodhidharma sat
in a cave for nine years. Two international Chan groups, Dharma Drum
Mountain and the Western Chan Fellowship, trace their Caodong lineage from Master Sheng Yen (聖嚴, 1931-2009) through Wansong and
Xueting.

Wansong's fourth dharma successor was Qingzhou (青州, n.d.),
the questioner in *Qingzhou's One Hundred Questions*, mentioned above.
Linquan says this about Qingzhou in his preface to that work:

---

13 Ibid., 234.

14 Jiang Wu, *Enlightenment in Dispute: The Reinvention of Chan Buddhism in
    Seventeenth Century China* (New York: Oxford University Press, 2008), 267-268.

Qingzhou, dharma ancestor, great master, grasps the essential teachings. A Caodong school innovator, he uses wisdom to arouse compassion, completely overflowing to his descendants.[15]

The fifth dharma successor of Wansong that I've been able to identify was a householder, Yelu Chucai, credited earlier for his role in the creation of Wansong's *The Record of Going Easy.* Yelu is mentioned in *The Whip for Moving Forward Through the Chan Mountain Pass*, a record of many inspirational stories of Chan attainment. This text was enormously important for Hakuin and continues as a popular manual for practice today. Yelu's section is titled "Powerfully Closing the Gate to Practice," and it says,

> Prime Minister Yelu Chucai practiced with Old Man Wansong, setting aside the duties of a householder, and ending the traces of people [coming and going]. Even though it was cold or hot and humid, there was never a day without practice. He worked continuously night and day. For almost three years, he abandoned lying down, and would forget to eat. Only then did he receive Wansong's seal of verification.[16]

Wansong died in 1246, leaving this death poem:

> Eighty-one years old
> only this one saying
> cherish and value all people
> and never make a false move[17]

Linquan Conglun and the One School

Linquan served as Wansong's attendant when Yuantong asked the one hundred questions and Wansong gave one hundred replies. As I shared earlier, sometime after the Q&A's, Linquan wrote one hundred verses to go with the question and answers of Yuantong and Wansong.

According to Steven Heine,

---

15 http://tripitaka.cbeta.org/X67n1313_001, trans., Dosho Port (unpublished).

16 *The Whip for Moving Forward Through the Chan Mountain Pass*, 禪關策進, Section 61, trans., Dosho Port (unpublished). Thanks for Kokyo Henkel for pointing this passage out.

17 八十一年 只此一語 珍重諸人 且莫錯舉, trans., Dosho Port (unpublished).

Linquan became a prominent figure during the early decades of the Yuan dynasty (1279-1368), who by citing various [koan] won a series of debates that were sponsored by Kublai Khan and held with Tibetan Buddhist and Daoist adversaries. He produced two seven-section pingchang collections based on case-with-verse texts initially composed by noteworthy Northern Song Caodong school predecessors. One is *The Empty Valley Collection* 林泉老人評唱投子青和尚頌古空谷集 (shortened: Kongguji) derived from odes by Touzi Yiqing (1032-1083), and the other is *The Empty Hall Collection* 林泉老人評唱丹霞淳禪師頌古虛堂集 (shortened: Xutangji) derived from odes by Danxia Zichun (1064-1117), who was the teacher of Hongzhi.[18]

You may remember that Danxia was the teacher of Lumen, whose lineage led to Wansong and Linquan, and of Zhenxie, an ancestor in the Caodong lineage that in a few generations led to Dogen and the Japanese Soto tradition. The fact that Linquan's two major literary accomplishments, *The Empty Valley Collection* and *The Empty Hall Collection*, involved several levels of commentary on the koans collected and verses written by two outstanding masters in the Caodong lineage, might suggest that Linquan's Zen was about uplifting only the Caodong line. This suggestion would be far from the truth about this great teacher.

In *The Record of Linji*, Thomas Yuho Kirchner notes that the version of the text that was probably published in the early 14th century was accompanied by a preface by Linquan.[19] This provides more spice to the history of *The Record of Linji,* a text with a long and sordid past. While searching the Chinese Canon for background on Linquan, I stumbled upon Linquan's *The Record of Linji* preface and was shocked and overjoyed by the energy of Linquan's praise for Linji. So first I'll share my ragged translation with you and then follow up with an explanation:

> The school of Caoxi [the Sixth Ancestor] is organized to purify what wells up and to share the inexhaustible flow. The Nanyue branch is majestic and lofty, and extends continuously without end, a vehicle like clouds piling up, with branches and leaves sprouting and thriving, nonstop shade for humans and gods, illuminating the Way of the ancestors.

---

18   Steven Heine, *Chan Rhetoric of Uncertainty in the Blue Cliff Record: Sharpening a Sword at the Dragon Gate* (New York: Oxford University Press, 2016), 234.

19   This is the record of Linji Yixuan (臨濟義玄, d. 866, Japanese, Rinzai Gigen).

No words express it. You must know "the meaning is not in the words." No scent is its scent. The fruit of faith is not having opinions. This all-inclusive principle, extremely incomparable, is its Way. Still, a thread remains, leaving an impact on those involved.

Thus, the founder, Linji, used the true dharma eye, the clear bright mind of nirvana. Great wisdom and great compassion flourished, turning the great pivot, applying the great function. His staff and shout completely cut off ordinary mind – a flash of lightning, a shooting star. At last, a harsh and sudden yank out of the secondary.

Then is a memorial recollection allowed? It is wrong to go to Korea wishing a phoenix will hurry to the heavens.

Not leaving a subtle footprint, passing and escaping through the profound barrier, through the three realms, bewildering disciples, Linji returned to the one true absolute reality. Under the heavens, his brilliance flowed and there were none who didn't gaze upward with admiration as he became the One School's ancestor with principle just as it should be.

Now, Chan Master Xueting, eighteenth generation descendant of Linji, pulled [*The Record of Linji*] together. I had searched Hebei [near Beijing] and Jiangnan [south of the Yangtze]. Then by accident the original arrived from Yuhang [in southern China]. Like a poor person obtaining a jewel, like being in the dark and obtaining a lamp, I leaped and jumped around cheering, extremely grateful. I gave away the cloth for robes, so that I could set up printing blocks and distribute [the *Record*], giving to all the various Buddhist monasteries this one extraordinary thing. Truly, so very rare! Look!

Reject the golden sound of the four oceans and know with certainty these pearls of wisdom with value difficult to repay.

Virtuous Mongol Dynasty, second year, second forty-fourth year in the sixty-year cycle; Dadu [modern Beijing], Bao-en Chan Monastery, abbot, successor of the ancestors; the solemn preface of Linquan Old Man Conglun, washing hands, burning incense.[20]

---

20 T47n1985_001 [0495a05], trans., Dosho Port (unpublished).

The first point in this effusive preface is the connection Linquan makes with Caoxi, the sixth ancestor, and his seventh generation successor, Nanyue (南嶽懷讓, 677-744, Japanese, Nangaku Ejo) to the eleventh generation successor, Linji, all "illuminating the Way of the ancestors."[21] But Linquan was not alone in his generous praise of the Linji succession. In the *The Record of Going Easy*, "Case 13: Linji's Blind Donkey," both Hongzhi and Wansong, Caodong masters in the other branch from the sixth ancestor through Qingyuan Xingsi (青原行思, 660-740, Japanese, Seigen Gyoshi, Green Source Walking Contemplation), compare the transmission from Linji to Sansheng (三聖, n.d.), to the transmission from the fifth ancestor, Huangmei (黃梅, 601-674), to the sixth ancestor, Huineng. In the following verse by Hongzhi, Wansong's capping phrases are in italics:

> At midnight, the robe of transmission[22] was handed to
> Huineng
> *A thief's son has the thief's knowledge*
> Disrupting and confusing Huangmei's 700 monks
> *The central beam is not straight*
> Linji's single branch of the true dharma eye
> *Half bright, half dark – all completely here now*[23]

In the second paragraph of Linquan's preface, "… the meaning is not in the words" (意不在言), is a direct quote of a line from one of the Caodong founders, Dongshan Liangjie, and his *Jewel Mirror Samadhi*. The next line of the Dongshan's poem, "but a pivotal moment brings it forth" (來機亦赴) is hinted at as another point of connection between Dongshan and Linji. Here we have the ancestral founders of both the Caodong and Linji lineages singing the same tune.

Linquan then summarizes the abrupt teaching style of Linji, and how he strongly emphasized the primary. Linquan wonders, tongue in cheek, if it's okay, then, to slip into the secondary and eulogize the great teacher.

Linquan then cites the monk who got the new *The Record of Linji* published, Chan Master Xuetang Puren (雪堂普仁, n.d.), who also hailed from near what is now Beijing, and was also closely involved with the Mongolian rulers of the Yuan dynasty. It seems likely that Linquan and Xuetang would have been acquainted, and so it seems likely that Linquan's

---

21 Caoxi is also known as Dajian Huineng (大鑒惠能, 638-713, Japanese, Daikan Eno, Great Mirror Insight Genius).

22 信衣 is literally, "faith" + "robe."

23 Wansong Xingxiu, *The Record of Going Easy*, Case 13: Linji's Blind Donkey, trans., Dosho Port (unpublished). Huangmei (黃梅), is also known as Daman Hongren (大滿弘忍, 601-674, Japanese, Daiman Konin, Great Fulfillment Vast Patience).

search for *The Record of Linji* preceded Xuetang's republishing of it.

In any case, Linquan reports searching all over and not finding a copy of the *The Record of Linji*. Then a copy unexpectedly arrived from southern China, bringing him such tremendous joy that the old man jumped up and down. I imagine this joy was aroused because in *The Record of Linji* he recognized not only the depth and power of Linji's Zen, but also that it conveyed the same one dharma light that was transmitted to him through Wansong and the Caodong succession. This now brings tears to my eyes. Linquan even honors Linji with the highest of praise, calling him "the One School's ancestor."

Linquan then relates how he was so determined to get this text into the hands of practitioners that he sold off the monastery's stock of cloth, presumably for the making of Buddha's robe. This text, after all, is just the robe. This robe is just this text.

Earlier in Linquan's practice, though, probably before he'd had the chance to examine *The Record of Linji*, he seems to have had a less favorable impression of the Linji succession. But to explore this, I first need to share Linquan's preface to the present text, *Going Through the Mystery's One Hundred Questions*.

Linquan's Preface Revealing the Way

> Know that Caoxi's blood vein ran straight, honoring Kasyapa's parent, Shakyamuni Buddha, and Bodhidharma's genuine tradition, receiving and establishing majestic presence. Then from the Sixth Ancestor, five schools arose, and dharma thunder shook the core of the provinces.
>
> Buddha's sunlight overflowed from Deer Park. Its clouds and rain are still nurturing the grass. Yuantong raised one hundred questions to encourage students, wholeheartedly disclosing the ancestral Way of verification with speech suitably simple and with nondiscursive subtle intent. Students came forward to practice inquiry, peacefully holding their credentials behind their backs. The teacher distinguished how many horns were on their heads. Were it not for great talent, disaster would wash away the opportunity.
>
> At that time, Yuantong had not yet met Wansong, but one day by chance he met the master when the Venerable Teacher Wansong lived at Mahabodhi Monastery. Through the upright application of samadhi, Yuantong experienced supernormal cognition. After waiting

patiently to verify him, Wansong transmitted the dharma to him. Previously, Wansong had answered each of the one hundred questions in a pointed instant, to guide today's bewildered masses. In the eye there is muscle.

Linji's key for the warp and weft gets the mystery, yet his tongue had no heart. Yunmen's words turned everything into gold, yet he didn't grasp Dongshan's biased and true. Neither established pure and serene gain and loss.

Many study words. Disciples expend a great deal of effort. Bowing to such people, the feet suffer fatigue. Wansong held the tongs and mallet of an adept behind his head. Their tongues don't survive when stuck in this furnace.

Yuantong asked. Wansong instructed. It could even be said that Wansong exhausted his virtue by not denying Yuantong.

Unexpectedly, I, Linquan Conglun, heard this record, and by retelling it, disrespected the floating words. Indeed, I do not contribute to the ascendance of the essential tenets of the school or restrain the excessive talkativeness of the ancestral domain.

Over half of the verses combine common swamp songs from the past. By the record's end, you'll think it was written by Uncle Yong in order to implicate mom and dad, and get laughs from all sides. It is important to know the beginning and ending. Read aloud with wild passion. Stomp your feet as an explanation. How many of the monastery's sutras are unread in the autumn?

The ancestral Way's thorough-going search leaves nothing to depend on. The dull-witted self will be ashamed on the day of going-through, patiently using a fox remnant to repair a mink fur coat. Then state the meaning of your intention and depend on what this preface says.

Seizing the opportunity two days before the seventh day of the seventh lunar month. Linquan's preface revealing the Way.[24]

Like in his preface to *The Record of Linji*, Linquan begins his preface

24   https://cbetaonline.dila.edu.tw/zh/X1312, No. 1312-A 通玄百問序, trans., Dosho Port (unpublished).

establishing the connection of his teacher, Wansong, and the lineage of Zen adepts in China and India, beginning with Huineng, the Sixth Ancestor (aka, Caoxi), then back to Mahakasyapa and his predecessor, Shakyamuni Buddha, then roll forward twenty-eight generations to Bodhidharma. Since the arrival of these great teachers, the whole world has been shaken to its core.

Linquan shares the Buddha's sunlight as it becomes rain in China, and we are all nurtured equally. Wansong is a teacher of great talent, few words, and heartfelt intention beyond the divided mind. When we tuck away our credentials, and open to buddhadharma, the teaching exposes our true nature. Wansong could see if students met the world as one or two. Trust this person.

Yuantong had the great good fortune to meet Wansong and cultivate absorption and awakening (神通; or "supernormal cognition"). When the time was right, he received dharma transmission. Before all of that though, one by one, one hundred questions flowed from Yuantong. One by one, Wansong responded with trained and powerful insight for the benefit of living beings today.

At that point, Linquan gets sectarian, quite in contrast to his tone above in his preface to *The Record of Linji*. Linji and Yunmen, founders of two of the five main lineages of the classical period, were great teachers, but here Linquan finds Linji's words were too harsh, and Yunmen as not embodying Dongshan's Five Ranks that unpack the multifaceted relationship of the biased and the true which formed the heart of the Caodong (Japanese, Soto) School for generations.

Instead of offering useless talk about the buddhadharma, Wansong embodies it fully, not even sparing his virtue for the benefit of Yuantong and of us. Linquan happened to hear these exchanges and seized the opportunity to share them with us.

I've translated these questions and answers to the best of my ability and added commentaries too, hoping that this might contribute to the ancestral Way. I'm afraid, though, that like Linquan, I've disrespected the floating words and merely contributed to the excessive talkativeness of the ancestral domain.

So now, you can take it up. My advice is to read no more than one Q&A and commentary a day. Digest the teaching without contrivance in sitting, standing, walking, lying down. It's all about the true you, so you don't have to cling to it. Indeed, give it all away. Give the sound of the cicadas to the sound of the cicadas. The smile of your loved one to your loved one. Do something small for the common good.

Take your time. Breathe and enjoy the leisure of this lovely moment.

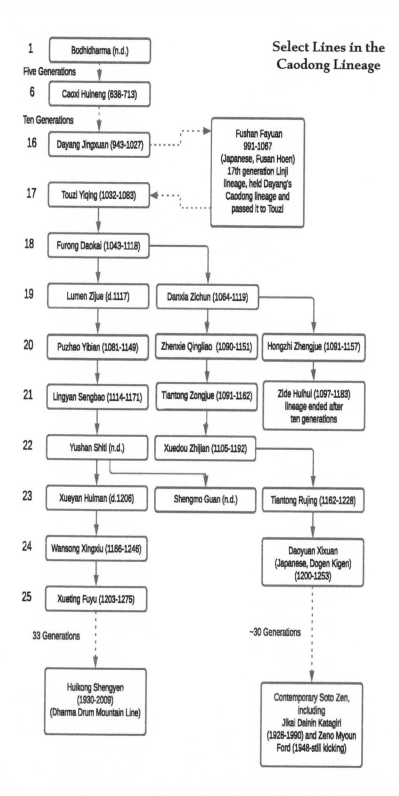

Select Lines in the Caodong Lineage

1 — Bodhidharma (n.d.)

Five Generations

6 — Caoxi Huineng (638-713)

Ten Generations

16 — Dayang Jingxuan (943-1027)

Fushan Fayuan
991-1067
(Japanese, Fusan Hoen)
17th generation Linji
lineage, held Dayang's
Caodong lineage and
passed it to Touzi

17 — Touzi Yiqing (1032-1083)

18 — Furong Daokai (1043-1118)

19 — Lumen Zijue (d.1117) — Danxia Zichun (1064-1119)

20 — Puzhao Yibian (1081-1149) — Zhenxie Qingliao (1090-1151) — Hongzhi Zhengjue (1091-1157)

21 — Lingyan Sengbao (1114-1171) — Tiantong Zongjue (1091-1162) — Zide Huihui (1097-1183) lineage ended after ten generations

22 — Yushan Shiti (n.d.) — Xuedou Zhijian (1105-1192)

23 — Xueyan Huiman (d.1206) — Shengmo Guan (n.d.) — Tiantong Rujing (1162-1228)

24 — Wansong Xingxiu (1166-1246) — Daoyuan Xixuan (Japanese, Dogen Kigen) (1200-1253)

25 — Xueting Fuyu (1203-1275)

33 Generations

Huikong Shengyen
(1930-2009)
(Dharma Drum Mountain Line)

~30 Generations

Contemporary Soto Zen,
including
Jikai Dainin Katagiri
(1928-1990) and Zeno Myoun
Ford (1948-still kicking)

Going Through the Mystery's One Hundred Questions

1

What place is smooth?

Yuantong asked: "Mysterious conduct is like wading through a rugged stream. What place is smooth?"

Wansong replied: "East. West. South. North."

Linquan's Verse

East West South North
Thistles and thorns invade the heavens
A stone person without legs
Has no need to labor
Even so, must pass through many double-mountain
    passes
At ease with the way of tangling the warp and weft

Commentary

Desperate for a smooth-going life, we come to dharma practice. Or press our thumb over the password reader for our handheld device. Or pull the cork from a bottle of Cabernet Sauvignon. Or make a program selection on Netflix.

And yet there's always something rough. A fly in the ointment. An ache in zazen. An annoyance on social media. A memory of a somewhat better Cabernet Sauvignon. A "haven't we seen this before?"

How can we go smoothly into the great good night?

In our Zen way, we take up wholehearted one-doing, also known as "mysterious conduct." Within the dynamic doing of vivid practice, conduct is intimate, mysterious, and a dark enigma. Each step, a step through the empty sky by the empty sky.

But *in* the vertiginous vicissitudes of daily life it is "… like wading through a rugged stream." Where can we find smooth-going?

I imagine Wansong pointing at himself from the four directions. "East. West. South. North." Going smoothly is coming from every direction and arriving together right here.

Like it or not.

As I work on these comments, I'm living on the north shore of Lake Superior, in an area that the Ojibwe called "Neyaashi." I walk the beach each morning after zazen with my wife and teaching partner, Tetsugan

Sensei. This fall morning, the leaves were just past their peak color and a strong southwesterly wind pulled so many to their next provisional destiny – to flow along the ground. The whistling wind, the rattle of the neighbor's wooden gate, the lapping of the waves, each whispers, "What place is smooth?"

Linquan's verse begins with his teacher's utterance (as they will throughout the *Hundred Questions*) and goes from there. "East West South North/Thistles and thorns invade the heavens." The invasion, the encroachment, of the heavens calls out about how the rough and smooth entangle. How in the soft warm mud, a relaxing day at the beach, for example, the thorns of an old relationship pattern reemerge. Or in blissful, quiet sitting, a memory of a hurtful word to a loved one suddenly pokes through the settled heart.

And yes, Linquan claims that "a stone person without legs/Has no need to labor." What's this about? "A stone person" is someone who's identity center has been cleared of attachment, the result of the persistent practice of mysterious conduct, the wrecking ball of Zen. Such a person has no legs, no eyes, no ears, no nose. And no need to get anything done.

Even so, there is the activity of compassion. How to liberate the many beings swirling like falling leaves in this world of suffering? There are so many of us, the colors so radiant, that the heart breaks and a wild cry comes forth. At the same time, there are no beings – just empty flowing phenomena. That conundrum is the "many double-mountain passes." How can we navigate such lofty, gut-wrenching terrain? How can we be "At ease with the way of tangling the warp and weft?"

The "warp and the weft" is a frequently used metaphor in the Zen literature of the classical period, referring to the fabric of life with all its bias and truth, vertical and horizontal, form and emptiness, as just one piece of cloth. The warp and weft are the cross-currents of this very rugged-stream life.

What place is smooth?

2

What is crossing over?

Yuantong asked: "In the dark, dark, dark place one must also exhale. Tell me, what is crossing over?"

Wansong replied: "At fault, but not repeating the offense."

Linquan's Verse

At fault, but not repeating the offense
A birding net at rest attends to much
Before the words "Good Morning!" – already a mistake
Error – then change your bearing
Ah! Ha! Ha!
Dark in darkest dark – what's to strive for?

Commentary

In samadhi, also known as concentration or absorption, the various vertiginous vicissitudes fall away. The whole body of the ten directions breathes the most subtle breath together, and the aspirant restrains from stirring the pot. To do so would be to make a mess of clarity.

This not-thinking is dark, mysterious, deep, and profound. However sublime – and such states can be the sublime of the sublime – they are provisional stages and not the illumination of buddhas and ancestors. They are states of grace, but not the saving grace. So what is crossing over?

Wansong's comment, "at fault," sees through Yuantong's restraint marked with control and contrivance. "Not repeating the offense," is to see and let go. Just once and not again.

When we rest the frontal lobe, suspending our cognitive skills' proclivity to divide and conquer, and instead allow the mind to open like a birding net at rest, the possibilities are limitless. With such subtle and profound awareness, even "Good morning" is crass and too much. Silence is too little.

Words and silence – just one mistake. Then simply change your bearing. Let go. Entrust yourself to the open birding net, laughing and singing spontaneously arising.

So intimate, who is striving for what?

This is not a rhetorical question.

3
Where is the one flower?

Yuantong asked: "'One flower, ten billion lands.' Tell me, where is this one flower?"

Wansong replied: "The unrefined place is also refined."

Linquan's Verse

The unrefined place is also refined
A stemless flower opens atop an iron tree
Sharp Zen practitioners set their sights on the lofty
Not like spring colors flattered Emperor Zhou

Commentary

"One flower, ten billion lands" is a phrase from *The Brahma Net Sutra*. Here is the context:

> Now I, Vairocana, sitting on the lotus flower platform,
> On the thousand petals that surround me a thousand
>   Shakyamuni's again appear.
> Each flower has ten billion lands, and in each land a
>   Shakyamuni.
> Each sits under a bodhi tree, and simultaneously they all
>   attain full enlightenment."[25]

Vairocana is one of the major Buddha figures in East Asia. *The Brahma Net Sutra* includes the Ten Grave Precepts and the Forty-Eight Minor Precepts. This system of Bodhisattva precepts is the precursor to Soto Zen's Sixteen Bodhisattva Precepts and would have been very well known to all practitioners at the time of this Q&A.

Perhaps fresh from a recitation of *The Brahma Net Sutra*, Yuantong asks where this one flower with ten billion lands is, each with a Shakyamuni Buddha attaining the way. It is, of course, right where divided seeing doesn't see it, in the nooks and crannies of greed, anger, and ignorance. Right here in our self-disparagement and/or self-aggrandizement.

---

25 *The Brahma's Net Sutra* (Taisho Volume 24, Number 1484), Trans., A. Charles Muller and Kenneth K. Tanaka, 41, https://www.bdkamerica.org/system/files/pdf/dBET_T1484_Brahmas_Net_Sutra_2017.pdf

Right here in our painfully self-centered actions. Look!

That is what Wansong means by "the unrefined place is also refined." How tender and fragile, how strong and indestructible! It defies all explanation, like a stemless flower blooming on the top of an iron tree. Like scooping up a random handful of sand and debris from a beach – bits of wood, glass pearls, plastic fragments, and, of course, sand. Refined or unrefined?

Those of you who are determined to realize the marrow of this one great life, stay focused on this essential point, and don't get distracted, dissipating energy on the flowers of adornment, the radiant mind of samadhi that arises as the fruit of diligent training. Or get intoxicated with the beauty of the buddhadharma.

That is the point that Linquan makes about Emperor Zhou – an early great emperor, reputed to be so virtuous that even the spring flowers would delight in complementing him.

Don't look off and get intoxicated by "One flower, ten billion lands!" Don't mistake being oh-so virtuous like Emperor Zhou with the wisdom gate of buddhas and ancestors!

Zen Master Dahui cautioned to Zen students saying, "You are always walking one step out in front of your own consciousness; you blind yourselves to the refreshing, lively, unrestrained basis right under your feet."[26]

"The unrefined place is also refined."

26　Dahui Pujue, *The Letters of Chan Master Dahui Pujue,* trans., Jeffrey L. Broughton and Elise Yoko Watanabe (New York: Oxford University Press, 2017), 242.

4
How can this be avoided?

Yuantong asked: "Hot as hell. Summer rain is like boiling water. Just now, how can this be avoided?"

Wansong replied: "Primary Mountain in front; Opposing Mountain in back."

Linquan's Verse

Primary Mountain in front; Opposing Mountain in back
At midday, gazing south at the Big Dipper
Blazing steaming hot weather – freely moving with the
    flow
After all, venerable, the problem is to become devoid of
    marks

Commentary

It's hot! It's cold! It's boring! My knees hurt! My back aches! Gotta pee!

It's always something, so in Question Four we return to the issue raised in Question One, the essential question of buddhadharma – how can all this suffering which marks human life be avoided? Crack this one and you'll plumb the depths of buddhadharma for sure. That will happen suddenly.

Practice it moment-by-moment and you've got something to write home about too. That will take just twenty or thirty years.

Yuantong seems to have had the following old case in mind in raising this question:

> A monk asked Dongshan, "How could one avoid the coming and going of cold and heat?" Shan replied, "Why not go to a place of no heat and no cold?" The monk asked, "What is it like, this place of no cold and no heat?" Shan said, "When cold, cold kills you. When hot, heat kills you."[27]

Where to go, where to go? Unfortunately, Wansong tells us where –

---

27   Yuanwu Keqin, *The Blue Cliff Record*, "Case 43," trans., Dosho Port (unpublished).

between a rock and a hard place. Fortunately, just hot and cold is where we are.

Wansong's reply here might seem especially cryptic. The Primary Mountain is the large mountain that faces the monastery. The Opposing Mountain is the large mountain that has the monastery's back. In between is just this person, just this heat, cold, ache, and piss. It can be avoided by dying to it completely. This is actualized by turning ourselves around, so that when we look south, we see the Big Dipper in the northern sky.

Then we can freely flow with like, dislike, and neutral. Just a-singing the one-doing ditty that is devoid of marks.[28] Killed by the heat. Killed by the cold.

---

28 For more on "devoid of marks," see *The Diamond Sutra*, trans., Muller: "If you see all characteristics to be non-characteristics, then you see the Tathagata." 若見諸相非相則見如來. http://www.acmuller.net/bud-canon/diamond_sutra.html#div-33

5

What single thing are you writing?

Yuantong asked: "The great ocean serves as ink. Mt. Sumeru serves as a brush. Tell me, what single thing are you writing?"

Wansong replied: "Going through the mystery's one hundred questions."

Linquan's Verse

> Going through the mystery's one hundred questions
> Not sticking to rhyme and rhythm
> At the last moment seizing the warp
> Everyone content with their part
> If someone asked me why?
> See how colorful language moves and turns the warp and
>   weft

Commentary

Just as myriad phenomena work together, none with a fixed nature, and the waves of the Great Lake lap at the shore, or roar at the beach, I set my fingers on the keyboard and earth, water, air, and fire (or whatever alchemical mix you prefer) as well as past, present, and future, act together. Inside, outside, and in-between arise thoroughly dependent, and these words come forth. Just as if the great ocean was ink for Wansong and Mt. Sumeru, the central axis of Buddhist cosmology, was his brush. What power!

More immediately, a few minutes before I started writing this I was working in the kitchen. Tetsugan hollered from the other room so that I'd know she was here, "Smelling good out there," referring, I assume, to the apple crisp I had just put in the oven. "All fall and spicy," she added, on this late October day, referring I guess to her favorite cinnamon spice that I added with wild abandon. It all comes together. And it'll all fall apart in a few minutes when we dish it up in healthy portions.

Yuantong's dramatic question, though, calling out so his teacher knew he was there, received a wry response from Wansong – a straightforward response with a striking sense of self-awareness. It gave me the giggles when

I first read it. The great ocean and Mt. Sumeru sure don't exclude giggles and hugs. Wansong, after all, was dictating *Going Through the Mystery's One Hundred Questions*, and so the brush was in Linquan's hand.

As for Linquan's part, he lets us know that his verses herein aren't going to fall into any pattern, and if you stay with us here, you'll find that they don't. Unlike the great Wumen's verses in his *No Gate Barrier*, there'll be no four-line verses with four or five characters each for Linquan! No way.

Seizing the opportunity together, Yuantong, Wansong, and Linquan, make each other. And thanks to the warp and weft, the intimate and universal, play along through colorful language. You and I can now stomp our feet and hold up our hands together as we clap along.

6

What realizes true nature?

Yuantong asked: "Observing a flower in the garden, one realized thusness. Now observing a flower, what realizes the true?"

Wansong replied: "Might as well ask the Sun God, but he will also not know."

Linquan's Verse

> Might as well ask the Sun God, but he will also not know
> "Not knowing" results in what?
> Not until your nose is deaf will you hear
> Just when you're blind as your eyebrows can you get a
> glimpse

Commentary

If there is no self, are you, like our friend Yuantong, wondering who awakens? Wansong has a bitterly honest, "Don't know," for you. Even the Sun God who created the flower that someone gazed at and realized thusness, who stares at the frantic human world from the perspective of the blinding sun, well, Wansong is sure he won't know either.

I am reminded here of something the twenty-seventh ancestor in the Zen lineage, Prajnatara, said when she (yes, "they" may have been a woman) was confirming her successor, Bodhidharma: "The flower opens and worlds arise."[29]

The flower has opened and worlds have arisen for many thousands of peope since the old Buddha walked the earth. "But what is it that awakens?"

Knowing this is beyond the ken of the divided mind. Realizing thusness depends on many factors, only some of which we can even influence, like a relationship with a teacher, skillful and diligent practice, careful study, active engagement in the welfare of others, and the chance oc-

---

29 Daoyuan, *Record of the Transmission of the Lamp*, vol. 1, *The Buddha and Indian Patriarchs*, trans., Rudolph S. Whitfield (Printed in Germany: Books on Demand, 2015), 134.

currence of seeing a flower in the garden in the early morning on one particular day. But who awakens with it?

Here a Zen student tells of their initial awakening experience in a garden:

> It happened in the middle of a difficult seven-day sesshin. I didn't know how I would go on. But somehow, I kept asking my bowls, the trees, and the toilet: what is *mu*? On the fifth day, I was sitting in the garden after lunch, inexplicably crying again. This time, I just let the crying be, and a huge wave of fear arose. The thought came: if I let go, who will catch me? I rode the fear, and the image of an outstretched hand appeared in my mind. I let go then and began to shake as waves of energy flooded my body. I disappeared and the world became luminous, each thing just exactly itself, impossibly vivid. The whole universe had always been boundless love, and I was overcome with gratitude.

Sometimes fear is the flower that opens into awakening.

Even the great masters, let alone mythological deities, cannot say what it is. They can just go with it in mysterious conduct. Dark. Dark. Dark.

Ah, but that sweet not-knowing! What does that result in?

This flower might just deafen your nose and blind your eyebrow.

Wait, though, isn't the nose already deaf and the eyebrow already blind?

7

What isn't pushed to change?

Yuantong asked: "Change pushes all living beings. Still, what isn't pushed to change?"

Wansong replied: "The motionless riverbank still confuses people."

Linquan's Verse

The motionless riverbank still confuses people
"True words" are likewise true
There are no accommodations for guests in the dragon tower
There are court ministers in the Imperial Palace
Get the mystery within the nondiscursive teaching
Praise the earth beneath your feet
Wish for a thoroughly intimate place
Exhausted nine times, again meeting spring

Commentary

In this fleeting world, do I get to keep anything? Is there something, anything, like a self, a soul, a feeling, or a perception that isn't pushed to change?

Right here we're already building a house on a floodplain and cheating ourselves and others. "Is there something that doesn't change?"

"Look for it here, folks! A self you can take with you to the grave … while you kick and scream."

The sixth consciousness looking at itself from the bank of the flowing river creates the illusion of permanence. Within the flow, the bank is moving. And yet, there's another level to this. Attaching to the teaching of impermanence can also become a motionless riverbank fooling people. Thus, the Buddha of *The Nirvana Sutra* taught,

> Blinded by defilement and ignorance, they create misconceptions in the form of inversions in their thinking: what is self they reckon as nonself, what is constant or permanent they reckon as impermanent, what is pure they reckon as impure, and what is joyful they reckon as painful. Because [living beings] are deluded by the

defilements, even if they recognize these [as errors] they still do not comprehend what this means, just like that intoxicated person who perceived something to be spinning when it was not.[30]

In other words, it takes a witness and an object to spin. When the object collapses into the witness, there is no heat, no cold, and no impermanence. That is to say, impermanence is the constant with no remainder and so is constant. When the Buddha disclosed this teaching, many of his disciples were shocked.

Constancy, joy, self, and purity also appear in the oft recited *Ten Line Kannon Sutra of Timeless Life*,

> Kanzeon!
> Namo Buddha!
> One with Buddha cause
> One with Buddha affinity
> Buddha, Dharma, Sangha affinity
> Constancy, joy, self, purity
> Mornings *nen* Kanzeon
> Evenings *nen* Kanzeon
> *Nen Nen* through arising mind
> *Nen Nen* not-apart from this mind.[31]

Likewise, when we are one with Buddha cause, one with Buddha affinity, we are constancy, joy, self, and purity stretching like a continuous river flowing for 10,000 miles.

Linquan's "True words are also true" (眞語), refers to the constant, clear teachings of the Tathagata – the motionless riverbank. From this perspective, we're all participants inside the Dragon Tower where there are no observers, no places to set up shop, and nothing to hold back. At the same time, in terms of active engagement in the welfare of others, like within the Imperial Palace, we are fully functioning with others.

A vital thing in this life, in this practice, is to clarify our mysterious intention to awaken and benefit all living beings. How did a boy from

---

30 *The Nirvana Sutra (Mahaparinirvana-Sutra)*, vol. 1, trans., Mark L. Blum, (Berkeley, CA: Bukkyo Dendo Kyokai America, Inc., 2013), 59. Also see *The Record of Empty Hall*, Case 14: Nanquan Offers New Tighty-Whities.

31 念 is "nen" in Japanese and "nian" in Chinese. Meanings including thought, memory, remembering, moment, mindfulness, and study. It is left untranslated here because there is no English word that covers these many dimensions. Trans., Dosho Port (unpublished).

the swamps of northern Minnesota like myself have the opportunity to do this work?

The causes and conditions are indeed mysterious. And undeserved. So, yes, indeed, I praise the great earth, the sun, the moon, and stars, and all the Buddhas and ancestors. And the Great Lake, oh, mercy, yes! Hallelujah!

It is the taste of the truly intimate place that keeps me going. Knocked down nine times, up and at it ten times. And repeat. Pushing change itself.

I'm so confused!

8

What doesn't change?

Yuantong asked: "The four seasons change. Still, is there something that doesn't change?"

Wansong replied: "Cold spring, warm autumn."

Linquan's Verse

> Cold spring, warm autumn
> Year after year – not separate
> A speck of dust in the blue-green ocean
> A snowflake on a red-hot stove
> Frosty leaves leisurely fall from a tree
> Rain passes, clouds withdraw, the sky is clear and pure

Commentary

Yuantong raises impermanence again, as if to say, "OK, in the last question I raised the issue of change within living beings and asked if there was anything left out. Well, how about in the natural world? Granted, seasons change, but is there anything that doesn't?"

We've just passed the point in the fall when the trees are at peak color here along the north shore of Lake Superior. We've been in a drought, so the colors have been muted and yet the hills, with hardwoods and evergreens, are splattered with golds, reds, deep greens, and vibrant yellows, all shuffling along in the cool north wind. Even though it's mid-October, we've yet to have a frost. Still, as I walked along the lake, I pull a wool hat down over my ears, and my eyes gaze out over the Great Lake to the vast horizon.

"Is there something that doesn't change?"

I say to Tetsugan, "I'm looking forward to a hot cup of Clouds-and-Mist green tea. How about you, my love?"

9

How is thusness meditation practiced?

Yuantong asked: "Searching for a teacher and investigating the path through meditation practice. How is thusness meditation practiced?"

Wansong replied: "For a long time, tending toward the wind of the Way."

Linquan's Verse

> For a long time, tending toward the wind of the Way
> Inner pattern and phenomena interpenetrate
> Every word prajna
> Each thing perfectly penetrates [Yuantong][32]
> It might have been a mistake to get right in his face
> Yet he turned towards the sun overhead and asked the
>   old man

Commentary

Studying Zen in Yuantong's time also involved finding a teacher and practicing meditation, 參禪 (Japanese, "sanzen"). The thusness meditation (如禪, Japanese, "nyozen") Yuantong asks about is one of four types of meditation identified in *The Lankavatara Sutra*, a key text especially in the early days of Zen in China, said to have been the text strongly recommended by the founder of Zen, Bodhidharma.

The four types of meditation are 1) the meditation for beginners, contemplating nonself, impermanence, suffering, and impurity; 2) meditation on dharmas, contemplating the nonself of self and other; 3) meditation on thusness, especially on the non-arising of thusness; and 4) Tathagata meditation.

Tathagata meditation:

> refers to enjoying the threefold bliss [from samadhi, enlightenment, and nirvana] that characterizes the personal realization of buddha knowledge and to performing inconceivable deeds on behalf of other beings upon

---

32 "Yuantong" means "perfectly penetrates".

reaching the tathagata stage.[33]

As for the third type, the subject of this inquiry, *The Lankavatara Sutra* does not give much more explicit instruction on precisely how to do thusness meditation, and thus Yuantong brings the issue to the appropriate person, his teacher. (There is no evidence in the historical record to suggest that he raised the issue on social media. Thank Buddha.)

Wansong offers guidance that might sound like step-by-step, gradual training: "For a long time, tending toward the wind of the Way." But this gradual training, as in Wansong's own personal experience, was initiated by a sudden breakthrough or two.

Then the wind of the Way (道風), the transforming power of the buddhadharma, especially the breath that is shared by a teacher giving guidance to their students, continues to open in unexpected and remarkable ways, even "performing inconceivable deeds on behalf of other beings," fulfilling the Great Vows to carry beings from the shore of suffering to the shore of liberation.

Thus, Wansong gives Yuantong advice to open himself to the wind of the Way of this dharma guidance. Yes, sometimes there are gale-force winds, sometimes the winds are oh-so-subtle that even the Great Lake perfectly reflects the deep blue of the sky.

A contemporary of Wansong in the Linji lineage, Wumen, offered this wind of the Way for working with the *mu* koan, a specific variety of thusness meditation:

> Do not do it as nothingness. Do not do it as yes and no.
> As if you've swallowed a hot iron ball – vomit and vomit
> but it won't go out. Wash away your former harmful
> knowledge and harmful feelings. Be skillful for a long,
> long time. Naturally, you'll succeed, breaking inside
> and outside. One day, you will be like a mute person
> dreaming – just allow self-knowledge.[34]

So even though both the Caodong and Linji lineages are sudden schools, in both expressions, it can take a long time, or even a long, long time following kensho (見性) to thoroughly and finally break inside and outside. Yet from the beginning, inside and outside, inner pattern and phenomena, interpenetrate, arising together in relationship, and are not another's business. Every word is it. You yourself are each thing.

---

33 *The Lankavatara Sutra*, trans., Red Pine (Berkeley: Counterpoint, 2012), 127-129.

34 Wumen Huikai, *The No Gate Barrier*, Case 1: Zhaozhou's Dog, trans., Dosho Port. (unpublished).

Illuminated by the one sun from before the empty eon, Yuantong took a risk to ask for instruction in such a central practice, the practice of how all things are – the non-arising of thusness.

Who are you?

10

Where did Guishan
turn into a water buffalo?

Yuantong asked: "Where did Guishan turn into a water buffalo?"

Wansong replied: "Beautiful black, fresh and green place."

Linquan's Verse

Beautiful black, fresh and green place
Difficult to find the inscription
Ask how [Guishan] plans to change
A sparrow hawk goes flying to Korea
Sing your moon song in the open pasture
Originally, the nose rope is broken
Hūm![35]

Commentary

Old-time Zennists, and apparently Yuantong too, loved the pickle about Guishan's water buffalo. It goes like this:

> Guishan is known to have said, "After I die, go down the mountain to a donor's house and you'll find me reborn as a water buffalo. On my left flank five characters will be written, saying, 'This is the monk Guishan.' At that time, would it be right to call the water buffalo 'the monk Guishan,' or would it be right to call him 'water buffalo'?"[36]

---

35 "Considered to be the generic seed of all deities in Esoteric Buddhism. It is often used in mantras and dhāraṇīs. It is composed from the four phonemes a अ, ha ह, u उ, and ma म. It means cause and is also said to signify thusness, from which all attributes are produced. Can also refer to the bodhi-mind, refutation, fulfillment of a vow, great power, joy and so forth." *The Digital Dictionary of Buddhism*, Thomas Muller, http://www.buddhism-dict.net/cgi-bin/xpr-ddb.pl?q=%E5%90%BD

36 Yuanwu Keqin, *Blue Cliff Record*, trans., Thomas Cleary and J.C. Cleary (Boston: Shambhala Publications, 2005) 160. Modified.

Water buffalo are domesticated beasts of burden and were very common in the agrarian world of the classical period of Zen. The water buffalo in the Zen narrative also represents buddha nature. Guishan, with no shortage of irony, wondered aloud about the function of a Zen master — are they domesticated beasts of burden or the wild and free buddha nature? To top it off, Guishan's successor at his mountain monastery was also named Guishan [Da'an].

Marge Piercy, a contemporary poet, might have responded,

> I love people who harness themselves, an ox to a heavy
>   cart,
> who pull like water buffalo, with massive patience,
> who strain in the mud and the muck to move things
>   forward,
> who do what has to be done, again and again.[37]

Doing what has to be done, again and again, Yuantong raises an intimate point, perhaps about his teacher, Wansong. Where did you become a domesticated beast of burden, following the schedule with the community of practitioners, giving dharma talk after dharma talk, student interview after student interview, answering one hundred questions and a hundred more? Where in your life was it that the buddha nature got so tame?

For me, round after round of zazen in Katagiri Roshi's zendo in Minneapolis.

For Guishan Da'an, it was like this:

> I've spent the last thirty years here on Guishan, eating Guishan's rice, shitting Guishan's shit, but not practicing Guishan's Zen! I just mind an old water buffalo. If he wanders off the road into the grass, then I pull him back by his nose ring. If he eats someone else's rice shoots, then I use the whip to move him away. After such a long training period he's become very lovable, and he obeys my words. Now he pulls the Great Vehicle, always staying where I can see him the whole day through, and he can't be driven away.[38]

For Wansong, it was a place that is "Beautiful black, fresh, and green,"

---

37 Marge Piercy, "To Be of Use" https://www.poetryfoundation.org/poems/57673/to-be-of-use

38 Andy Ferguson, *Zen's Chinese Heritage: The Masters and Their Teachings* (Boston: Wisdom, 2000), 124.

like in a fertile field in ancient China. But was it Wansong that got domesticated, or was it a water buffalo, or was it the buddha nature that got Wansong'ed?

Linquan also has a hard time reading the writing on the furry brute. All this where? And how? Certainly misses the point. Just singing in the rain, no ring knows the nose. How can it be clearly expressed in a way that is animal, human, and the buddha nature too?

If only there was some way, like a generic seed syllable. The sound of thusness from which all attributes flow. Something that is the sound of the water buffalo, but is neither human nor beast, something that seems to non-arise. Something so primordial that it is in itself the fruition of vow, great power, and joy.

Hūṃ!

11

Beating Buddhas and Ancestors

Yuantong asked: "Deshan was a descendant of buddha ancestors. If buddhas came around, they too would be beaten. If ancestors came around, they too would be beaten."

Wansong replied: "Not daring to be lazy."

Linquan's Verse

Not daring to be lazy
The sangha gathering is accustomed to it
Knowing kindness, repaying kindness
Mind-to-mind without any gap
Yunmen agreed to carry and uphold the true mandate
Flute sounds from the quiet river, the ocean is peaceful

Commentary

Deshan was famous for beating practitioners. For example, in *The Concordant Sounds Collection of Verse Commentaries*, a collection of classic koan with verse comments by three important female Zen masters, Case 30 is simply and in its entirety, "Whenever Deshan saw a monk enter the gate he would hit [them]."[39]

In our present case, Yuantong's question is implied – "What the hell?"

Miaozong, a successor of the great twelfth-century Linji master, Dahui, and one of the commentators of *The Concordant Sounds Collection of Verse Commentaries*, expresses the heart of the buddhadharma, like this:

> Today I, the mountain monastic, together with this world and all other worlds, with the buddhas and [ancestors], with the mountains, rivers and great Earth, the grasses and trees, woods and forests, appear before the fourfold assembly, each of us turning the great wheel of Dharma. Everyone's radiances blend and crisscross like a jeweled silken net. If there be a single blade of grass,

---

39   *Zen Echoes: Classic Koans with Verse Commentaries by Three Female Chan Masters*, trans., Beata Grant (Somerville, MA: Wisdom, 2017), 111-112.

a single tree, that does not turn the wheel of Dharma, then one cannot call my sermon today a true turning of the great wheel of Dharma. . . ."[40]

If so, why beat the hell out of everyone, even buddhas and ancestors?

Deshan's great enlightenment came when his teacher, Longtan, blew out a candle Deshan was holding, just as he hesitated to go out into the dark night. By beating everyone, it was simply Deshan's intention to blow out their candles with blows from his staff. He wouldn't even dare slight buddhas and ancestors. He wouldn't spare them the opportunity to illuminate subtle clinging and continue extinguishing the great Way.

And he continued right to his death.

Deshan was not well and a monk asked, "Is there someone who does not get sick or not?" The master said, "There is." The monk said, "Who does not get sick?" The master said, "Ouch, ouch!" Deshan continued, "You extend your hands to the sky and chase after echoes, exhausting your mind and body. Wake up from the dream and realize it was not. In the end what is there to do?" Once [Deshan] was done talking he sat peacefully and passed away.[41]

But we haven't quite finished with Deshan's wanton beatings. Miaozong versifies them like this:

> Killing and bringing to life simultaneously:
> The poison and the Dharma nectar together.
> Is it a punishment? Is it a reward?
> Your guess is as good as mine![42]

Linquan is less ambivalent. "Seeing kindness, repaying kindness," refers to what Deshan received from Longtan and what he then bequeathed to his successors, one of whom, a generation later, was the great Yunmen, who held up staffs, shitsticks, darkness, the kitchen, and the main gate.

Do you hear the "Flute sounds from the quiet river?" Do you know "… the ocean is peaceful?"

Ouch! Ouch!

May you also receive the kindness of Deshan's blows.

---

40 Ibid., 14-15.

41 *Collected Works of Korean Buddhism, vol. 7.1*, Gongan Collections I, Case 609, trans., Juhn Y. Ahn (Seoul, Korea: Jogye Order of Korean Buddhism, 2012), 609.

42 Op Cit., Grant, 111.

12

When an Ancestor comes, he shouts – Why?

Yuantong asked: "Linji was a descendant of buddha ancestors. Yet, when buddhas came, he shouted. When ancestors came, he shouted. Why?

Wansong replied: "Just because buddhas come, ancestors come."

Linquan's Verse

> Just because buddhas come, ancestors come
> How to avoid conjecture?
> I now am you
> The crossroad rumbles open
> If perhaps not yet, trust the true remedy
> Still more, suddenly hear thunder shaking nine
>   boundaries
> Hey!

Commentary

In the previous question, Yuantong raised the beating feature of the Zen narrative and here, as a complement, covers the issue of shouting. So let's look to the *The Concordant Sounds Collection of Verse Commentaries* again for our source on this well-known attribute of Linji (Japanese, Rinzai) from Case 26 "Linji's Shout":

> When Linji saw a monk enter the gates, he shouted.[43]

Buddhas, ancestors, monks, you and I, all avoid conjecture together. Hey!

The true remedy, thunder shaking the barriers, the crossroads crumbling open – all from that wholehearted Linji shout.

Deshan, in the last chapter, picked up his knack for beating people from his teacher Longtan blowing out his candle. Linji picked up his knack for shouting from getting a good beating:

---

43 Ibid., 102-103.

Linji asked Huangbo, "What is the buddhadharma's really and truly big idea?" Bo then struck. After three times, [Linji] took leave of Bo [and went to see Dayu]. Yu asked. "Where are you coming from?" Ji said, "Coming from Huangbo." Yu said, "What words and phrases did Huangbo have?" Ji said, "Somebody asked three times about the buddhadharma's really and truly big idea. Three times, suffered the stick. Don't know how I didn't get along." Yu said, "Huangbo's this way? Like an old grandmother embracing [you]. Still, you come and ask what you didn't know – how you didn't get along." With these words, Ji arrived at great realization.[44]

What is the buddhadharma's really and truly big idea? And did Huangbo share it with Linji or not?

In either case, Miaozong offers this verse:

> Bellowing and shouting, railing away
> With the energy of ten thousand men.
> Discuss the Buddhadharma,
> And you will still miss your move.[45]

What is it that's missed?

Might be as close as those buddhas and ancestors just coming and going.

---

44 Wansong Xingxiu, *The Record of Going Easy*, Case 86: Linji's Great Realization, trans., Dosho Port (unpublished).

45 Op Cit., Grant, 102.

13

The same or different?

Yuantong asked, "Zhaozhou pointed to a cypress tree. Buddha raised a flower on Vulture Peak. Tell me, are these the same or different?"

Wansong raised two fingers.

Linquan's Verse

> Raise two fingers
> Establish order
> Let go of everything you've been carrying
> Nothing more
> During the first lunar month, stop forcing out-of-season
>   growth
> Do not be showy like a reckless moth

Commentary

The question here relies on two koans for the set-up. First, Zhaozhou was asked by a monk,

> "What was the Ancestral Teacher's purpose in coming from the West?" Zhou said, "Cypress tree in the courtyard."[46]

And second,

> When the World-Honored One was at Spirit Mountain with the assembly, he twirled a flower in front of them. Everyone was silent. Only Mahakasyapa broke into a little smile. The World-Honored One said, "I have the treasury of the true dharma eye, the wonderful mind of nirvana, the true form of no form, and the subtle gate of the teaching. I now entrust this to Mahakasyapa."[47]

---

46 Wumen Huikai, *The No Gate Barrier*, Case 37: Zhaozhou's Cypress Tree in the Courtyard, trans., Dosho Port (unpublished).

47 Ibid., Case 6: The World-Honored One Twirling a Flower.

Yuantong asks if these cases are the same or different. Well, they do both have horticultural references, but that may not be what Yuantong was getting at.

Zhaozhou was responding to one of the most common questions in the koan literature, "What is the meaning of the ancestral teacher, also known as Bodhidharma, coming from India to share the dharma in China?" Bodhidharma knew that there was no place to go and no one to save, and yet at an advanced age, he endured the rigors of ocean travel to do what he could to establish wholehearted awakening in a foreign land. What was his intention? His inner, subtle meaning? And what does pointing to a tree have to do with it?

What is the meaning of the buddhadharma coming into your life?

The Buddha raised a flower and his student's face broke into a smile. It seems this form or no form, the subtle blown-out mind, doesn't mind having many faces. What was Mahakasyapa smiling about? Did you smile or not?

So, the question here is if Zhaozhou's pointing to a tree and the old Buddha raising a flower the same or different?

Wansong raised two fingers. Does this mean that he sees the tree and the flower as the same or different? Is Wansong raising two fingers the same or different from Zhaozhou's tree or the Buddha's flower? Or do the two fingers represent the tree and the flower?

This is the discipline. Letting go of nothing more and nothing less than everything we're carrying. It can't be forced. It can't be delayed.

Enormous energy arises from this release.

And yet, don't be like a reckless moth!

14

Who can enjoy it?

Yuantong asked: "Dongshan's place of no cold and no heat – who can enjoy it?"

Wansong replied: "Sensation like the stone statue in Jia Prefecture."

Linquan's Verse

Sensation like the stone statue in Jia Prefecture
Raise an eyebrow
Force shut the empty sky
No bias, no friends
The way of handing down the many pleasures of the
    heart
What use is a horse's bridle?
Make offerings of blooming flowers

Commentary

In this question we return to an issue that was raised in "Question 4: How can this be avoided?" with an even more direct reference to Dongshan's no heat, no cold. The full koan, once again, goes like this:

> A monk asked Dongshan, "How could one avoid the coming and going of cold and heat?" Shan replied, "Why not go to the place of no heat and no cold?" The monk asked, "What is it like, this place of no cold and no heat?" Shan said, "When cold, cold kills you. When hot, heat kills you."[48]

The repetition is essential, because this is really the heart of the matter for any dharma student: what is freedom from suffering? The Zen method of identity action points the way: "When cold, cold kills you. When hot, heat kills you."

That's a handy skill when living in inhospitable climates like where I live now and, if not in your locale yet, it's likely to be coming soon.

---

48   Yuanwu Keqin, *The Blue Cliff Record*, Case 43, trans., Dosho Port (unpublished).

Northern Minnesota is cold in the winter, so cold that it can overwhelm the senses, take the breath away, and close down the throat, but if you do spew something out, it may well freeze before it hits the ground. Then the stiflingly humid heat in the summer drains vigor from all but the mosquitoes.

When killed by heat and cold, that is, when there is no separation, no witness, just the world of heat or just the world of cold in all ten directions, who is it that could enjoy it? Doesn't enjoyment require a witness? It's not that there is no one, of course, and being it is believing it.

So Wansong presents a barrier that's 71 meters (233 ft) tall, the Leshan Great Buddha (乐山大佛), reputed to be the largest and tallest Buddha statue in the world. Carved out of a rock cliff from Cretaceous red bed sandstone between 713 and 803, it is a depiction of Maitreya, the future Buddha. This is the stone statue in Jia Prefecture.

Zhongfeng Ben said,

> All you must do is make your mind like wood or stone and your thought like dead ashes. Take this earth, water, fire, and wind illusion body and cast it beyond the worlds of the other directions. Trust entirely to whatever happens – even if you're ill, it's okay; even if you're brought back to life, it's okay; even if you die, it's okay.... In the midst of these sorts of sense fields you're not shaken at all, just urgently take up the keyword which has no tastiness, and, silently inquire on your own."[49]

Who can enjoy sensation like that?

Like Linquan, you might raise an eyebrow here, embodying the futile effort to shut out empty space. However, the *who* that enjoys being killed by heat and cold, isn't apart from our liking this person and disliking that person.

How can this way of the heart be shared? At some point, the techniques of control become the subject of inquiry. What use is the bridle and whip? Instead, offer something beautiful to the world, like "... flowers blooming on a distant mountain to the Tathagata ... offering treasures you had in a former lifetime to sentient beings."[50]

49 *The Chan Whip Anthology: A Companion to Zen Practice*, trans., Jeffrey L Broughton and Elise Yoko Watanabe (New York: Oxford University Press, 2015), 103.

50 Eihei Dogen, *Treasury of the True Dharma Eye: Zen Master Dogen's Shobo Genzo*, "The Bodhisattva's Four Methods of Guidance," trans., Kazuaki Tanahashi (Boulder: Shambhala Publications, 2010), 473.

15

How would you scale the peak of wonder?

Yuantong asked: "One must scale the peak of wonder straight up to pass through. How would you scale such wonder?"

Wansong replied: "There is hardship in serious dharma."

Linquan's Verse

> There is hardship in serious dharma
> Play with being a transformed person
> Your grasp on wonder blows away like a feather
> Unify ten thousand nations
> Pass through the many worlds not concerned about a
>   speck of dust
> You should know that the function of true completion is
>   no function

Commentary

I first heard the phrase "peak of wonder" while studying *The Blue Cliff Record*, Case 23, with Katagiri Roshi in the early 1980's.

> When Baofu and Changqing were walking in the mountains, Baofu pointed, saying, "Just this exactly is the peak of wonder." "Yes, but yes ...," said Changqing, "What a pity."[51]

I loved the flashy immanence of Baofu's pointing, "Right here. Right here." And his dharma friend, Changqing's sardonic, "What a pity." As it happened, Katagiri Roshi gave a talk on this case just as I was getting some actual experience with the peak of wonder. I craved for some direction on how to go straight up and through, just as Yuantong notes here, and with no small sense of the waggish, asks how to scale wonder.

How can one travel up and through that which is not apart from the right-here-right-now ten-direction self? I listened to the cassette tape of

---

51 Yuanwu Keqin, *The Blue Cliff Record*, Case 23, trans., Dosho Port (unpublished).

Roshi's talk probably a hundred times looking for some clues.

In Yuanwu's *Blue Cliff Record* commentary to this koan, he gives some backstory. The "peak of wonder" comes from *The Avatamsaka* Sutra, in *The Flower Ornament Scripture*'s final book, Book 39: "Entry Into the Realm of Reality." In that book, a lay seeker, Sudhana, undertakes an extensive dharma pilgrimage, visiting one hundred cities and fifty-three teachers. Sudhana is presented as a role-model for us as he inexhaustibly digs into the depths of the buddhadharma, learning from whoever can teach him, regardless of whatever demographic category he might put them in – old and young, monastics and householders, humans, and nonhumans, and so on.

Certainly, as Wansong reminds us in the present study, there is hardship in such serious dharma practice. The contrast between Sudhana walking with straw sandals through one hundred cities and finding fifty-three teachers, without Google Maps even, and the ease with which we can engage a teacher and community by flipping open our laptops and joining a Zoom session, could not be starker.

Sudhana began his dharma pilgrimage with an encounter with the bodhisattva of nondual wisdom, Manjusri, who referred him to Meghasri bhiksu. Here is how Yuanwu presents the story of their meeting:

> In the teachings it says that Meghasri bhiksu stayed on the lone summit of the peak of wonder. He never descended the mountain. Sudhana went to join him, searching for seven days without finding him. How did they happen to meet? Nevertheless, when they were together, Meghasri said, "All buddhas' radiant wisdom shines everywhere. The dharma gate is met everywhere."
>
> Since Meghasri never descended the mountain, why meet on a separate peak? If you say he descended the mountain, within the teaching it says Meghasri bhiksu never descended the mountain. He was always here at the lone summit of the peak of wonder. Yet Meghasri was together with Sudhana. Where could they definitely have met?[52]

Meghasri was always on the <u>lone</u> summit, how could he have met somebody else? How could Sudhana have met somebody who was always alone? How can we scale such a conundrum? Indeed, there is no space to pretend when embracing the peak of wonder or it will blow away like a non-proverbial feather.

---

52 Yuanwu Keqin, *The Blue Cliff Record*, Case 23, trans., Dosho Port (unpublished).

Linquan lends a lifesaving hand: "Unify ten thousand nations/Pass through the many worlds not concerned with a speck of dust." He may be thinking here of Sudhana, passing through one hundred cities, ten thousand nations. Unify it all! Stop the fighting on the other side of the river!

Where can we find energy for the long and winding road? The very scope of this work is one source for refreshment. We are traveling through many worlds, our little blue green dumpling planet zipping along at incredible speed: the Earth at the equator rotating at ~1000 miles per hour, revolving around the sun at ~67,000 miles per hour, our solar system revolving around the galactic center at ~514,000 miles per hour, and the Milky Way is traveling at ~1.3 million miles per hour compared to oldest stars in universe.

"How would you scale such wonder?"

Yuanwu pulled the words of Elder Li out of some dark place to illuminate, prefacing his verse with this:

> Elder Li surely tied some entangling vines, and tied them good.
> The way of the lone summit of the peak of wonder
> Is a single taste – everywhere the dharma gate
> One by one each and everything is true
> One by one each and everything is complete
> Turn toward no gain and no loss
> Completely expose the place of no yes, no no
> Therefore, Sudhana could not meet[53]

---

53 Ibid.

16

What is not-two's nature?

Yuantong asked: "Wisdom and ignorance, their nature, not two. What is not-two's nature?"

Wansong replied: "'Doesn't show at daybreak.'"[54]

Linquan's Verse

'Doesn't show at daybreak'
Dragon song, foggy night
Words avoid completion
The essential pivot mutually turns
The light of the sun on the vast ocean longs to clarify
    illumination
Beginningless, yet, suffering the soft smoke of jealousy

Commentary

"The sound of chanting and the sound of farting," Katagiri Roshi once observed, "have the same not-two nature. And yet each has its own virtuous qualities."

So too with wisdom and ignorance. Both are empty of themselves through and through. And yet each has its own virtuous qualities.

As if following up on "One by one each and everything is true/One by one each and everything is complete" from Elder Li's verse quoted in the last chapter, Yuantong asks, "What is the nature of nonduality?"

Wansong's response harkens back to a line from a seminal verse by the founder of the Caodong lineage, Dongshan Liangjie, *The Song of the Jewel Mirror Samadhi*. It is still recited frequently in Soto Zen centers in the West and in Japan, some forty-four generations later. Here is the line "Doesn't show at daybreak" with a little company around it for context:

Midnight truly bright;
doesn't show at daybreak.

Make this the standard for the sake of living beings;
it's use uproots all dukkha.

---

54 Dongshan Liangjie, *Jewel Mirror Samadhi*, trans., Dosho Port (unpublished).

Although unconstructed;
it is not that which has no words.[55]

What is it that is truly bright at midnight, but doesn't show in the light of a new day, in the light of dividing consciousness? Someone might say, "Well, that would probably be the no nature of not-two."

Sure. You bet. It's rolling in like the dragon's song on a foggy, foggy night, like the Superior Bay Lighthouse, just down the point from us, casting its light in a misty, misty morning.

Yet, that isn't clear enough. What is it that's singing that song? Is it chanting or is it farting?

As for "completely avoiding words," Dongshan's Japanese successor Keizan, just sixteen generations later, wrote,

> One can only proceed by utterly cutting off the faculty of mind, such that white scum forms at the edges of the mouth. This does not mean that words are to be shunned or that silence is to be commended. It is simply to let you know that your mind is 'such'. It is like pure water, like empty space. Making it pure and clear, this is 'interpenetration without obstruction.'[56]

That's the dark. What about the light? What about "The essential pivot mutually turns/The light of the sun on the vast ocean longs to clarify illumination"?

Keizan continues:

> Have you not seen the saying, 'every person's singular radiance'? In its brightness, it is like the shining of a thousand suns arrayed together. Those who are ignorant face outwardly and seek it, but those who are clear-sighted face inwardly and do not think about it.[57]

Oh, I wish I could express the dharma as clearly as Keizan!

"Beginningless, yet, suffering the soft smoke of jealousy."

---

55   Dongshan Liangjie, *Jewel Mirror Samadhi*, trans., Dosho Port.

56   Keizan Jokin, *Record of the Transmission of Illumination*, trans., William M. Bodiford (Tokyo: Soto shu Shumucho, 2017), Volume 1, 91.

57   Ibid.

17

How to reach the Way's inner pattern in a single leap?

Yuantong asked: "'With one leap, directly enter the Tathagata stage.' How about you? Say how to reach the Way's inner pattern in a single leap."

Wansong replied: "Embrace this earthen urn's flow."

Linquan's Verse

Embrace this earthen urn's flow
How noble is a good plan!
Begin with trust in pure craving to be always content
Thus we know thick mud of much sorrow
Arrive at a place where you can take your cut of the
    winnings
and take your cut of the winnings

Commentary

The Caodong lineage, represented here by Yuantong, Wansong, and Linquan, has always been within the stream of practice of the sixth ancestor's sudden enlightenment. Rather than proceeding baby-step by baby-step, taking almost forever and a day until you get there, the spirit of Zen is to reach the Way's inner pattern, the Tathagata stage, the sweet and luminous truth of this life, in a single leap.

At the same time, in Great Vehicle Buddhism, there are a wide array of schemas for dharmic development, including the Ten Stages of the Bodhisattva:

1. Joyful
2. Immaculate/stainless
3. Luminous
4. Radiant
5. Invincible
6. Immediacy/coming face-to-face
7. Far-reaching/transcendent
8. Immovable/steadfast
9. Eminence/auspicious intellect

10. Cloud of dharma.[58]

Then the eleventh stage, the Tathagata (thus come one) stage (aka, "universally luminous"), is referenced here by Yuantong. How is it possible to leap from the confines of a sniveling, angry, horny, large-brained primate to suddenly enter the stage of a Tathagata?

"Embrace this earthen urn's flow."

The Tathagata stage might seem so far away, and yet it is so close – just this earthen urn, just this body. The character for earthen urn, 瓮, also designates an urn with ashes of a dead person. It also is just this close.

And yet, if you plan to go there, even if there is here, you can expect the "thick mud of much sorrow." Instead, oh Universally Luminous One (yes, that's you!), collect your winnings. Right now.

The doors of the bank of the casino-of-life-and-death are wide open.

---

58   Robert E. Buswell and Donald S. Lopez, Jr., *The Princeton Dictionary of Buddhism* (Princeton and Oxford: Princeton University Press, 2014), 1086.

18

What conditions "no-place-not-known"?

Yuantong asked: "Prajna and ignorance. What conditions 'no-place not-known'?"

Wansong replied: "Do not slander another's good."

Linquan's Verse

> Do not slander another's good
> A skillful explanation is not equal to the direct way
> Just talking can cut off the subtle mystery
> Then see the mind contriving the unproduced
> Towering, towering, flying, flying self-thus faith
> Sweep through the dead leaves of past positions

Commentary

Juxtaposed with prajna and ignorance, Yuantong asks what conditions 無所不知, no-place-not-known, aka, omniscience.

Today, within a close teacher-student relationship, Yuantong might hear, "Oh my goodness, you are so in your head!"

I can still feel the sting of the verbal blows dished out by Katagiri Roshi to the young Dosho. With sadness in his eyes, seemingly wondering if he was wasting his life with students like me, he muttered almost to himself, "That's just your thinking. Always."

Wansong begins his ancient scolding by pointing out that asking about omniscience, acting like he does not know, is itself slander of Yuantong's original inheritance.

Linquan takes it from there, saying that talking about "no-place not-known" is a betrayal of the mystery.

But, thankfully, we are not left there.

Linquan points his index finger straight at the moon: "Towering, towering, flying, flying self-thus faith."

"Self-thus" is the keyword here with "faith" slathered on for good measure. Towering, towering, 兀兀, originally referred to a table mountain and now means "determined," "unmoving," or "steadfast." Dogen also used this binomial, for example, in his *Healing Point of Zazen*, along with 地, meaning "earth" or "ground," so the phrase is translated as "steadfast sitting," or "fixed sitting." This phrase is a crucial teaching in

Dogen Zen. "You should," says Dogen,

> investigate and receive the authentic transmission of steadfast sitting. This is the thorough study of steadfast sitting transmitted in the buddha way.[59]

Linquan, though, rather than pair "towering, towering," 兀兀, with 地, "ground," pairs towering with "flying, flying," 腾腾, for a much more dynamic expression.

In modern Chinese, the whole sentence, "Towering, towering, flying, flying self-thus faith," sounds like this: *wùwù téngténg xìn zìrú*. But remember, "Just talking can cut off the subtle mystery."

The invitation here is to embody the <u>self-thus</u>, towering and flying, and immediately, intimately "Sweep through the dead leaves of past positions."

---

59   Eihei Dogen, *Treasury of the True Dharma Eye: Zen Master Dogen's Shobo Genzo*, "The Point of Zazen," trans., Kazuaki Tanahashi (Boulder: Shambhala Publications, 2010), 303.

19

What is the one push?

Yuantong asked: "'Push open the closed window of illumination.' Tell me, what is the one push?"

Wansong replied: "Just now is the new place."

Linquan's Verse

Just now is the new place
Wonderful to go through the difficult-to-grasp mystery
Grasp the hawser, freeing the boat
Buy a hat for one another's heads
Were it not for the sun revealing the heart's yearning
Who could press from both sides to make the mountain
range the gate for the main hall?

Commentary

What is the one push that opens the window of illumination? Wansong replies that the window is already open. And yet. The initial part of the Zen journey is about *not* accepting this on faith, but instead to make this experiential discovery for oneself. One of our central methods was most clearly articulated by Dahui, just a century before Wansong's time – the keyword method, especially with the keyword *wu* (Chinese) or *mu* (Japanese). And, yes, "no" or "non" in English also serves this practice nicely.

One of the most just-now-is-the-place skillful teachers in recent Japanese history was Nagasawa Sozen Roshi (1880-1971). In this chapter, I'll go into some detail of the kensho experience of a woman who worked with Nagasawa Roshi to convey the wonder of going through the difficult-to-grasp mystery.

Nagasawa Roshi trained with Harada Sogaku Roshi, one of my dharma ancestors, and received transmission from him. She then started the Tokyo Center for Nun's Training and guided many women, monastics, and householders, who pushed open the window of illumination, including Harada Tangen Roshi who did his first of several sesshins with her, and also eventually became a successor of Harada Daiun Roshi and the longtime master of Bukkokuji.

Sixty stories of those who experienced kensho under Nagasawa Roshi are collected in *Sanzen Taiken Shu* (*A Collection of Meditation Experiences*).[60] Unfortunately, the full text has not yet been translated, but a summary of two women's kensho experiences appears in an essay by Sallie King, "Awakening Stories of Zen Buddhist Women." I'll focus on just one.

King writes,

> [Nagasawa Roshi] is depicted as being quite stern and even fierce with her disciples before they make a break-through in their practice, shouting at them and abrupt-ly ringing them out of the interview room with her dismissal bell; she relies heavily on a koan practice in which the disciple aggressively assaults the ego, suffering a roller-coaster ride of blissful highs and despairing lows in the process ....

One woman who entered training with Nagasawa Roshi was Nakayama Momoyo, whose only son had been killed in the war. "I was pushed," she recounted about his death, "from a world of light into a world of gloom. I lost all desire to live; every bit of happiness was taken away in grief and hopelessness."

Eventually, she heard a talk by Nagasawa Roshi:

> My hard heart was shut tight, leaving me without a soul in the world to turn to. However, as I listened to the talk, and was touched by her character, I felt somehow that there was dragged out from me some kind of inno-cence free of poison which was just on the other side of my deep and relentless bitterness.

Nakayama began sesshin practice and was eventually assigned the *mu* koan. She repeatedly entered Nagasawa Roshi's dokusan room to present her understanding, only to be met with rebukes like these: "Don't spout logic! It's just your ego!" "That's emotion!" "That's theory!" "That's inter-pretation!" "What are you waiting for?" "That's a hallucination!" "That's just a belief!" "That's just an idea!" "That's just a blissful feeling!"

Her kensho came when she forgot all about dokusan,

> I went out into the yard and quietly sat down. Before the temple house one great tree stood alone, reaching to the clouds. In harmony with my chant of Mu—,

---

60 Iizuka Koji, ed., *Sanzen Taiken Shu* (*A Collection of Meditation Experiences*), with a Foreword by Nagasawa Sozen (Tokyo: Chuo Bukkyosha, 1956), pp. 30–38 and 242–46.

Mu—, Mu—, the earth trembled and urged me on. Azalea leaves and small flowers spoke to me one by one. The bright moon laughed and became one with me. Night passed. How pleasant the morning practice, how sweet the little bird's song! The crisp crunch, crunch, crunch of the tenzo at the cutting board, the sound of the mallet as a woman out back hammered away cracking soybeans – from everywhere I could hear wonderful, indescribable music.

Nakayama had entered into a blissful and wondrous *mu* absorption (samadhi) but had not yet pushed open the window. In dokusan, she was met by Nagasawa Roshi's ferocious roar and was sent back to her zafu to continue the work. After some time,

A tiny insect flew onto the paper door; it was Mu. An airplane flew through the sky; it was Mu. The whole universe was nothing but Mu. In the midst of this, the wooden frame of the paper door fell away and vanished. My body felt as if it were being dragged up from deep within the bowels of the earth. "Gong!" rang the temple bell, and suddenly, I cried out and returned to myself. It was attained! "Heaven and Earth are of one piece. The universe and I are one body. I am the Buddha! We're joined in one!"[61]

Who could press from both sides to make the mountain range the gate for the main hall?

For one, Nakayama Momoyo, that's for sure. Another, seven hundred years before, was Yuantong of whom Linquan reported in his preface to this volume, "Through the upright application of samadhi, Yuantong experienced supernormal cognition."

So, I'm thinking, we might all buy hats for one another's heads.

---

61 *Buddhism in Practice*, edit. Donald S. Lopez Jr. (Princeton, NJ: Princeton University Press, 2007), 404-405.

20

What is our country?

Yuantong asked, "Although Chang'an is hotly disputed, our country is certainly quiet. What is our country?"

Wansong replied, "In the midst of hot dispute."

Linquan's Verse

> In the midst of hot dispute
> No obstructions for a clear-eyed adept
> Sit, observe the clamor and the quiet raising and falling
>   together
> Seize heaven and earth, manifest the sacred era

Commentary

I've been wondering "What is our country?" too. As I write this, in June of 2022, there seem to be at least two countries sharing the same space – one vaccinated, very concerned about the climate crisis, and generally supportive of President Biden while the other seems hell-bent on turning back many of the living being-positive reforms of the past fifty years.

What is our country?

I imagine, dear reader, that you too, in whatever time and place you are reading this, have similar concerns.

Meanwhile, on most days, most people get up and take care of what needs to be cared for – getting food on the table, kids to school, work done as well as possible, the house as clean as can be, and the dishes ready for the next meal. At the same time, both those on the political right and the left wonder, "Who have we become?"

These concerns were certainly shared by the ancients as well.

Linquan, in his *Empty Valley Collection*, sites this old case to test a novice monk:

> "I hear Chang'an is very noisy; do you know or not?"
> The novice said, "My province is peaceful." Yaoshan asked, "Did you realize this from reading the scriptures or from making inquiries?" The novice said, "I didn't get it from reading scriptures or from making inquiries." Yaoshan said, "Many people don't read scriptures

or make inquiries – why don't they get it?" The novice's whole body was hands and eyes – he wouldn't be tied up or overthrown; he said, "I don't say they don't get it – it's just that they don't agree to take it up."

Linquan commented, saying, "If you can forget both clamor and silence, you will surely understand the simultaneous realization of absolute and relative."[62]

Chang'an, the ancient capital of the southern division of what had once been the unified China, was a noisy place of hot dispute even in the best of times, a place full of the hustle and bustle of human life.

In Yuantong's time, though, the Mongols, led by Genghis Khan, had invaded northern China and threatened to conquer the south as well, a feat they eventually would accomplish. A high minister in the northern court, a man named Yelu, had served the previous rulers of northern China, and successfully transitioned to become a high minister for the Khans, serving them as well. Yelu was also a close student of Wansong, (see the Introduction for more) and is credited with convincing Genghis Khan to win over the population rather than slaughtering many as had been the Khan ways. Yelu must have been quite the adept!

But what is *our* country? Or as Yaoshan put it, "Do you know or not?"

It is *in* hot dispute. And to find our country, to know or not, that's where we must be as well. Going into hell, even, like Jizo Bodhisattva. When we see clearly, the circumstances are not obstructions.

To help us make this the vivid, living truth, Linquan has some specific pointers.

First, sit!

Second, look! Observe how the noise and the quiet arise and fall away together.

Third, "Seize heaven and earth, manifest the sacred era." In other words, take the bull by the horns! Then we all drop off.

At just such a time, we have the opportunity to uplift the just-now, self-thus circumstances with this very body-mind through sitting, standing, lying down, and walking. The sacred is precisely this very conflicted, mundane place.

In the midst of hot dispute.

---

62 *Timeless Spring: A Soto Zen Anthology*, trans., Thomas Cleary (New York: Weatherhill, 1980), 80-81.

21
Still teaching or not?

Yuantong asked: "Matanga's future is this world. Is he still teaching or not?"

Wansong replied: "Staying is definitely not the Way."

Linquan's Verse

Staying is definitely not the Way
A bamboo staff searching grass shadows
The first rank white horse
Established the standard for mowing rice
Then and now, palm leaves are effective when words
    vanish
Do not follow words and phrases, giving rise to misery

Commentary

In the Chinese story about how the buddhadharma came to China, Matanga and Zhu Falan are central figures. According to which, about 2000 years ago, the Emperor Ming had a dream about a golden man and sent emissaries to find him. Those who went west, along the Silk Road, found two monks, Matanga and Zhu Falan. The emissaries returned with these monks who made a lasting impression by riding into the capital on pure white horses. The emperor built a monastery for them and named it the White Horse Monastery. Matanga and Zhu Falan are credited with translating the first text into Chinese, *The Sutra in Forty-two Sections*, although this sutra is now considered to have been written in China and the two monks are regarded as legendary figures.

Yuantong's question is about whether the teaching of the ancients has continued until his day. And I wonder if it has continued until ours. Zen, particularly, is an ancestral tradition, based on the transmission of the buddhadharma from heart to heart from the Buddha until today. What about the helpless ones in the future? Will the living buddhadharma be transmitted to them?

In our day, the number of students doing monastic practice has fallen to a level that probably has not been seen since the early years of Shakyamuni Buddha's teaching career. As for Japanese Zen, as close as I can figure, there are a few hundred in the US and about 400 in Japan – both

Soto and Rinzai.

A Zen monk friend recently told me about doing a 90-day practice with an old Korean monk who told him repeatedly, "The task of this generation is to blow out the candles."

That is, the monasteries are closing down, so blow out the candles on your way out. If the buddhadharma is to be transmitted to future generations, it appears most likely to occur through householders, rather than monastics. And it isn't clear if householder practice offers the depth and clarity of awakening that's necessary for transmission.

I told this story in my Zen teachers group and a week later, a teacher friend confided in me that it's still coming up for him. He told me, "Everytime I remember 'blow out the candles,' I get chills through to my bones."

"Staying is definitely not the Way."

Everything changes. Everything. That's the one constant, a theme that we explored in Questions 7 and 8. Searching outside of ourselves for something constant in love, career, or possessions is like taking a pole and poking at shadows in the grass.

Matanga and Zhu Falan on their white horses raised the bar of transmission high up through their translation work (for which "mowing rice" is slang, given that Chinese characters look like scattered grains of rice). After all, when the spoken words and the living examples of the ancients fade away, it is better to have the written transmission on palm leaves, paper, or digitally, than nothing. It is still better to be unattached to words and texts.

Attachment to tradition also gives rise to misery.

22

There is still Zen, no?

Yuantong asked: "Bodhidharma's future is this earth – there is still Zen, no?"

Wansong replied: "Staying is exactly the Way."

Linquan's Verse

> Staying is exactly the Way
> His voice illuminates vastness
> Do not mistakenly haggle about the dharma
> Stop separating, searching through discussion
> Stop searching through discussion
> The tips of willow branches have no sour dates

Commentary

Bodhidharma was the founder of Zen in China, probably in the early sixth century. He is often referred to as simply *the* Ancestor. Whether a myth or a "real" person, the legacy of Bodhidharma is essential to the Zen narrative. As the story goes, after he met his teacher Prajnatara, he awakened and then served her for many years. Following her death, he taught for many years and finally following her instructions from early in his life, he headed off for China to share the dharma, although he was already a centenarian.

After a harrowing voyage on sea and land, he arrived in China and got an audience with the Buddha-heart emperor named Wu. It did not go well, so instead of having a big impact in a short period of time as might have been the case with imperial support for his teaching, Bodhidharma crossed the river into northern China and sat in a cave near Shaolin monastery, gazing at a wall for nine years. Eventually, he found one disciple and the Zen way of sudden awakening slowly spread across the vast land of China. And seven hundred years later, Wansong's lineage would inherit the abbacy at Shaolin and they are still there now, more than seven-hundred-and-fifty years later. We will return to Bodhidharma in "Question 29: What is Bodhidharma's usefulness?", "Question 33: What is the essence of mind?" and "Question 80: Disclosing Zen insight."

In this chapter, the question: Is staying the Way or not?

In the previous chapter, Wansong taught that "Staying is definitely not the Way." The very next words out of his mouth were, "Staying is exactly the Way." So which is it?

To frame it another way, with what mind is there no contradiction?

The sound of a teapot hissing in the kitchen is the vast voice of Bodhidharma reverberating still, even here in what we're calling the Neyaashi (Ojibwe for "point of land") Zen Hermitage in northern Minnesota.

How can a sober person hedge, wiggle, and haggle this? It is not a matter of discussion with others or yourself. Really.

Be like a willow branch. When cut, you can insert the end into the soil. If there's decent drainage and a bit of moisture, roots appear. As the willow branch is established in this new place and becomes what we call a tree, on the tips of the branches, buds suddenly appear. Those buds are very likely to be willow buds, not sour dates.

"Enlightened people of today are exactly as those of old."[63]

---

63 Eihei Dogen, *Eiheikoso hotsuganman*, trans., Dainin Katagiri (unpublished).

23

Why does it seem to be secure, not leaking?

Yuantong asked: "The boat has no bottom, so why does it seem as if it's secure, not leaking?"

Wansong replied: "Forged in pig iron."

Linquan's Verse

> Forged in pig iron
> Not heavy, not light
> Secure, not leaking
> Not entering the billows, roaming the depths of the
>   ocean of original nature
> All living beings pass through the five murkinesses of
>   degenerate ages

Commentary

We know that this body is made up completely on non-body elements and so is vastness itself. Such a body is dependent, not secure. And when we gaze at the starry, starry night, we know this world is vast and wide. This leaky, insecure, vast boat, in other words, has no bottom. So, what the heck is this about pig iron and what does it have to do with the conundrum of our individual existence in a world that is vast and wide?

Let me explain. The name for pig iron comes from the appearance of how it is molded. It happens to look like a litter of piglets being suckled by a sow. The Chinese started smelting pig iron sometime before 250 BCE, about 1500 years before the Europeans. The metal produced by the pig iron process is brittle and with few direct uses. It is important, though, as an intermediate product as it is ideal for producing more highly refined irons that have many uses. Even the ancient Chinese, though, were probably not making iron boats in the 13th century, so pig iron here is a metaphor.

Wansong's point is that the sense that things are stable and Yuantong's question itself are intermediate products – not heavy, not light – with a bitter-sweet sense of melancholy that might be suitable for a good poem. But as a dharma inquiry, it isn't yet using the base stuff of this life to forge a Great Way, although that is a possibility for Yuantong. Wansong's observation seems to have been offered as a simple fact.

We all have to go through the many murkinesses of this life – like the five murkiness mentioned in the verse, those caused by the age we're living in (indeed); murkiness caused by our mistaken ideas; murkiness caused by how we get triggered by greed, anger, and ignorance; murkiness of just being a living being; and the murkiness caused by having an ever shortening life ahead.

So, there are many reasons to hold our fellow traveler, Yuantong, ourselves, others we meet on the road, and the pig iron of this life with a most tender touch.

24

Whom did Yanguan tell to bring the rhinoceros fan?

Yuantong asked: "Whom did Yanguan tell to bring the rhinoceros fan?"

Wansong replied: "Already carrying profound intention."

Linquan's Verse

Already carrying profound intention
It'd be good to remember such words
The attendant's mouth dropped open
How to hold hesitation?
Stop waiting! Today is the day of the bright moon
Change direction! A cool breeze circles the earth

Commentary

I better break this one down.

The Rhinoceros Koan:

> One day Yanguan called his attendant, "Get me my rhinoceros fan." The attendant said, "The fan is broken." Guan said, "Since the fan is broken, bring back the little rhinoceros." The attendant had no answer.[64]

Such a simple, everyday situation. The teacher, Yanguan (750-842), one of Mazu's many illuminated successors, calls for his fan, which apparently is broken. But the teacher is actually looking for the real thing, not the human contrivance. And we're left with the attendant's painful hesitation.

Who is called to get the fan? Who is broken? Who hesitates and how? And what about the rhinoceros fan?

The stuff of the Zen training environment is not stuff. Just as in the process of training where we take ordinary human beings and make them buddhas, the stuff of training is carefully crafted from grasses and trees, soil and earth, like old man Dogen said,

---

64   Yuanwu Keqin, *The Blue Cliff Record*, Case 91, trans., Dosho Port (unpublished).

Together, the grasses and trees, soil and earth of the place touched by this cultivation of the Buddha way radiate a great light, and preach the profound and mysterious dharma without end. The grasses and trees, fences and walls manifest the teaching for all beings, common people as well as sages, and they in turn extend this dharma for the sake of grasses and trees, fences, and walls. Thus, the realm of self-and-other awakening invariably holds the true form of full realization, and realization itself manifests without ceasing for a single moment.[65]

The grasses and trees, the stuff of this life, turn the dharma wheel! So, a great deal of attention has been given in Zen to such stuff, the transmogrified grasses, trees, fences, and walls. Steven Heine said this about one anthology of Zen stuff in China:

> The twenty-volume *Classified Anthology of the Chan Forest* (Ch. Chanlin lieju) is an early fourteenth-century compendium of Chinese koans, verses, and commentaries that are organized into over one hundred categories. It includes classifications for passages about apparel and footwear, various implements, the zither and chess, curtains, boats and vessels (vol. 15), whisks and hammers, prayer beads, tin bottles, walking sticks, bamboo hats, mirrors, door panels and fans (vol. 16), household utensils, swords, bows and arrows, antiques (vol. 17), and incense and lamps (vol. 19)....[66]

So for detailed questions about fans, I'll refer you to the *Classified Anthology of the Chan Forest*, vol. 16.

In our present investigation, the grasses, trees, soil, and earth have been transmogrified into a rhinoceros fan (Japanese, seigyo senshi, 犀牛扇子), one of the symbols of transmission used by a Zen teacher, whether it is hot or cold. In addition, the rhinoceros fan may, sadly, or may not be made of rhinoceros bone and may or may not have calligraphy or a drawing connected with a rhinoceros on the face of the fan. The rhinoceros fan is an implement for the Zen teacher who wanders free and solitary like a rhinoceros. Like expresses like.

Within this context, Yanguan calls for his rhinoceros fan. The free

---

65 *Zen and Material Culture*, edit. Pamela D. Winfield and Steven Heine, "Materializing the Zen Monastery," Pamela D. Winfield (New York: Oxford University Press, 2017), 55.

66 Ibid., "Introduction: Zen Matters," Pamela D. Winfield and Steven Heine, xvii.

and solitary one calls to whom? You might be inclined to dip into some dharma babble here about no one calling and no one answering, but this certainly will not transmogrify grasses and trees to radiate light. What will? Who is called?

Wansong uses the opportunity to complete the previous chapter's call and response where we're left neck deep in the five murkinesses, by pointing out that even though the attendant can't pick up the rhinoceros fan and bring it to him because something is broken, he is the one who is "Already carrying profound intention."

Before the broken one leaves, the wild rhino arrives.

Thus, the key to actualizing the buddhadharma is in how to be hesitation. In the midst of delusion, the Way radiates great light. Although it may well be dark, dark. Don't hesitate about hesitation! Just die with hesitation.

"Stop waiting! Today is the day of the bright moon/Change direction! A cool breeze circles the earth."

25

How many years did it take Zhaozhou to make a seven-pound robe?

Yuantong asked: "How many years did it take Zhaozhou to make a seven-pound robe? The return smashes *mu* to bits as well."

Wansong replied: "One turn pulls out, one turn pushes in."

Linquan's Verse

> One turn pulls out, one turn pushes in
> The grasping fingers of the hands of faith employed most
>   intimately
> The whole one hundred twenty years of gathering and
>   lifting
> Even now, as before, not apart from this body

Commentary

In our day and going back at least to Hakuin in the 18th century, this koan has been taken up after a student has kensho'ed – abruptly embodied nonduality. And by the way Yuantong frames the issue, it appears to have been used this way in his day, five hundred years before Hakuin, and in the Caodong lineage, no less. But before we get to Yuantong's presentation, a bit about the koan he is referencing:

> A monk asked Zhaozhou, "Ten thousand dharmas return to one. Where does one return?"
>   Zhou said, "When I was in Qingzhou I made one cloth robe weighing seven pounds."[67]

Zhaozhou here is Zhaozhou Congshen (778-897), a tenth generation successor in China of the great Nanquan. Zhaozhou is known for his gentle way of "lip Zen." Light emitted from his mouth when he spoke, and he didn't resort to shouting or beating, like some people. Zhaozhou didn't settle down to teach until eighty years old, and then lived on until

---

67   Yuanwu Keqin, *The Blue Cliff Record*, Case 45, trans., Dosho Port (unpublished).

one-hundred-and-twenty. This is probably historically accurate and not a Zen fishing story. Koan cases involving him, including the *mu* koan, occur repeatedly in all the major collections.

No one says more clearly how to work with Zhaozhou's Qingzhou Robe koan than Hakuin:

> These words can work with a marvelous effectiveness. If you take them and apply yourself to them in your practice, if you bore into them when you are meditating and when you are engaged in daily activities, when you are walking, standing, sitting, or lying down, bore into them from the sides and from the front and from the rear, and continue boring into them until there is no place left to bore, no place to put either a hand or foot, nothing whatever you can apply thought or understanding to …

Let's pause here to highlight the significance of what the old master is offering – a method for unrelenting application of one's original kensho, that all things return to one, but then what? In my case, from the first time I heard this koan from Katagiri Roshi until about twenty-five years later when I worked through it with James Myoun Ford Roshi, it haunted the bejesus out of me. I had had some taste of awakening, then eventually received dharma transmission in Katagiri Roshi's just-sitting lineage, and then even began teaching. If I ran across this Zhaozhou's Qingzhou Robe koan in a Zen book or newsletter, I'd feel nauseous and ashamed from head to toe. Clearly, I hadn't penetrated "where does one return?" let alone Zhaozhou's Qingzhou robe.

I found from bitter experience that it is essential to work through this in face-to-face encounters with a skilled teacher. If you attach to feelings or a divided mind even in the slightest, you won't pass through. If you cling to belief in any understanding of the buddhadharma, you might well be inflicted with a painful bout of Zen sickness. Fortunately, by the time I dug into this, I'd learned to just follow the advice of my teacher, and was fortunate to verify that when continually boring into it, as Hakuin put it,

> … at that time, if you keep pushing steadily forward without faltering, the time will come when everything suddenly falls away and satori opens up. The joy you experience at that time will be something you have never known before. No beneficial act you could perform would produce a result of such magnitude.[68]

---

68   Hakuin Zenji, *Complete Poison Blossoms from a Thicket of Thorn: The Zen Records of Hakuin Zenji*, trans., Norman Waddell (Berkeley, CA: Counterpoint, 2017), 383.

In the process, as Yuantong pointed out from what must be his direct experience, any remaining taste of one's initial kensho, represented here by *mu*, will of necessity, desperate necessity, be smashed as well, in the very process of sewing the Qingzhou robe. Only then will there be a taste of thorough-going freedom.

When asked, "Ten thousand dharmas return to one. Where does one return?"

Zhauzhou said, "When I was in Qingzhou I made one cloth robe weighing seven pounds."

When *mu* is smashed to bits, and the "return" is clear and bright, the immediate meaning of the Quinzhou robe will be clear and bright as well. But how long will it take to get there, that is, to get here? How long will it take to make this seven-pound robe?

Wansong's response and Linquan's verse both come from knowing how it is to sew a robe, stitch by stitch. "One turn pulls out, one turn pushes in." That's how long. There is no time, because it is right here, in the return to this very body itself.

Linquan brushes away any remaining obscurities: "The grasping fingers of the hands of faith employed most intimately/The whole one-hundred-twenty years of gathering and lifting."

26

Who is able to hear it?

Yuantong asked: "A mud ox bellows at the moon. Who can hear it?"[69]

Wansong replied: "The eyebrows of a person with leprosy."

Linquan's Verse

> The eyebrows of a person with leprosy hear the fruit of
>   falling off
> In the night, Sumeru is startled, stands up, and rides the
>   clouds
> Intimate friends need not hold each other up again and
>   again
> Clearly, eight ounces are half a pound

Commentary

Let's begin by unpacking some of the images. First, an ox made of mud represents the messiness of our afflictive emotions and how they tend to be splattered all over our environment, affecting our family, friends, and things.

Second, "A mud ox bellowing at the moon" represents the realized person braying with the subtle moonlight of illumination. Third, the phrase that I've translated as "A mud ox bellowing at the moon" is just four characters: 泥牛吼月, *mud ox bellows moon*. While the classical Chinese characters invite a wide range of possible relationships in tune with the experience of Zen, English invites a specificity in relationship between parts of the phrase that limit directionality of the relationships. If there's someone bellowing we want to know who it is and what they're bellowing at. "Mud ox bellows moon," opens the field of possibilities. The mud ox could be bellowing the moon. The moon could be bellowing the mud ox. The mud ox could be mud bellowing the mud ox, bellows could be bellowing the bellows, and the moon could be mooning the moon.

The realized person bellows the moon. So Hakuin described the sixth

---

69 This and the next chapter work with images that appear in *The Record of Yuanwu.* Thanks for Kokyo Henkel for pointing this out.

ancestor as "A mud ox barging headlong into a boiling surf."[70] This is our life. Bellowing our truth, barging in the boiling surf, dissolving into the great ocean with no trace. Is it awakening? Is it death? The one choice seems to be if we barge headlong or go kicking and screaming.

Who hears your bellow?

I recently asked some students what phrases they have really heard me bellow, and they replied: "That's it!" "Just be *mu*." "Cool story, what's the living reality?" "Ok, and how does this show up in your life?" "What would be another way to express it?" "More intimate!" "Important!" "Show me only one *mu* in the whole universe."

Such is the life of a Zen teacher. Who can hear?

Wansong leaves it to "The eyebrow of a person with leprosy." Leprosy was quite common in ancient China, and still today there are about 200,000 cases reported annually worldwide, many in India. As in the Mideast and Europe, those with the disease in ancient China were marginalized and discriminated against. So Wansong identifies the downtrodden leper with the mud ox. Both having bits and pieces falling away with no hold on the identity center.

The eyebrows themselves, when falling off, hear the sound of liberation. Even the mountains dance, and our intimate friends on the Way, those who hear the music just like we do, don't hold us up, but let it all fall down. "Intimate friends," 知音, by the way, will come to visit again in "Question 43: Is this guest or host?" and "Question 60: Where is enlightenment's exquisite flowering?"

For now, it's enough to see that we're all made of the same empty stuff. Eight ounces is half a pound.

---

70 Hakuin Zenji, *Complete Poison Blossoms from a Thicket of Thorn: The Zen Records of Hakuin Zenji*, trans., Norman Waddell (Berkeley, CA: Counterpoint, 2017), 438.

27

Who hears liberation?

Yuantong asked: "A wooden horse neighs. Who unexpectedly hears liberation?"

Wansong replied: "Futile to wipe the corner of your eye."

Linquan's Verse

> Futile to wipe the corner of your eye – turn, enter into
>   empty hearing
> Ten thousand sounds soar – the source of the self is
>   settled
> Hearing sound, examine the inner pattern – stop
>   expending great effort
> As before, a soaking rainfall turns the summit blue-green

Commentary

The mud ox, the stone woman, the wooden man, and here, the wooden horse all represent a non-thinking person of true activity, thus, a symbol of Zen emancipation. Neighing is a location marker for horses when communicating with humans and can be heard almost a mile away. It is sign of separation anxiety, social isolation, or paradoxically, delight. Here it is like bellowing at the moon, embodying true expression. Like Dogen said (modified),

> Because active buddhas manifest awesome presence
> in every situation, they bring forth awesome presence
> with their body. Thus, their transformative function
> flows out in their [neighing], reaching throughout time,
> space, buddhas, and activities.[71]

This neighing of aloneness is the Buddha's "I alone am the World-Honored one." So, no need to dry your tears. Let the warm tears of compassion flow by turning into empty hearing. What kind of hearing is that? In the hearing, just the hearing.

---

71 Eihei Dogen, *Treasury of the True Dharma Eye: Zen Master Dogen's Shobo Genzo*, "The Awesome Presence of Active Buddhas," trans., Kazuaki Tanahashi (Boston: Shambhala Publications, 2010), 260 (modified).

Lay down your weary tune, lay down, and just embody the inner pattern. Be the flowing tears.

"As before, a soaking rainfall turns the summit blue-green."

28

How much did you practice?

Yuantong asked: "A three-legged donkey practices walking with a makeshift hoof. Tell me, today, how much did you practice?"

Wansong replied: "Do not go about in confusion."

Linquan's Verse

> Do not go about in confusion
> Falling into the weeds, he speaks about who is without
> Still more, especially stop asking about faults and errors
> Consider realizing faults and errors

Commentary

Some days, like yesterday, as I deal with the body falling apart (plantar fasciitis, a tooth ache, oh, my goodness), I felt like a three-legged donkey with a makeshift hoof, hobbling around the Zen barn, moaning and groaning. I definitely did not feel much like a mud ox bellowing at the moon, or a wooden horse neighing. How about you? How is your practice going?

Such a question certainly falls into the weeds and assumes that there are good days and bad days, gain and loss. Nothing wrong with that because there certainly are. But nothing right with it either because there certainly aren't.

A student with some taste of awakening recently wrote in a Vine forum,

> I'm still obsessed with thoughts about *me*. I bet I go through all 500 koans and am still like this. Sometimes I am able to look at that *thought*, not as fact, but as an expression of someone who can't trust in the process/teacher/group. But sometimes, something will come up and I am not so sure about where I am. Maybe I'm progressing in fits and starts and in ways not always easily measurable, that my over concern with *me* is part of the problem – not part of the solution.

Yeah, so don't go about confused. Instead of just rolling around in bed all night wondering, "Where did I go wrong, where did I go wrong?", you might just direct your energy to realizing the true nature of your faults and errors.

Realizing? The character that's translated here as "realizing" is 成 which has several dimensions of meaning. 成 can mean to accomplish or perfect, so in that sense, you might say, "Today I'm going to accomplish my faults and errors!" 成 also means fulfillment or consummation. So "Today I'm going to consummate my faults and errors!" And 成 means realize as in becoming buddha. So, "Today I'm going to realize my faults and errors and become buddha."

You don't have to change a thing.

29

What is Bodhidharma's usefulness?

Yuantong asked: "A hornless iron bull hibernates at Shaoshi. Tell me, what is its usefulness?"

Wansong replied: "A humble Fudo Son."

Linquan's Verse

A humble Fudo Son
Radical reason should be maintained
Down, unfathomably, is up
Who dares to argue?
In the land of no yin or yang there is no crossing over
A peasant's sloppy presentation breaks off a body part

Commentary

Shaoshi is another name for Bodhidharma, the great founder of the Zen Way in China. See "Question 22: There is still Zen, no?" for more on that useless, hornless iron bull. He's a living legend for his radical nondual reason, he's also just an old dead guy, and he's someone who is still causing problems as scholars and heady Zen students argue about his historicity. What good is he?

Wansong likens him to a humble Fudo Son (Chinese, Budong Zun; Sanskrit, Aryacalanatha). Fudo Son is a wrathful dharma protector, often depicted sitting in flames with sword in his right hand cutting off delusion, and a lasso in his left hand, capturing those little doggies so that they can be hogtied. Like this old Indian monk with no eyelids covering his blue eyes, red hair, and wild attitude, sitting for nine years at Shaoshi. How's that for the framing of our great ancestor who maintained and transmitted radical reason?

"Radical reason" 道理, could also be rendered the "Way's inner pattern." I owe "radical reason" to the great scholar, Hee Jin Kim.[72] Radical reason is the beating heart of the great matter of birth and death. Radical reason arises when you've turned yourself around so that down is up and unfathomability unfolds through you. Right here there is no light and dark, no secret and exposed, no female and male, and no transcending

---

72 Hee Jin Kim, *Dogen on Meditation and Thinking: A Reflection on His View of Zen* (Albany, NY: State University of New York Press, 2007).

these dualities. Just radical reason. Then you've got 80 percent of it.

You can't blame Huike, the second ancestor, for cutting off a body part, his arm, in awe. Or exasperation.

Give the man a hand.

30

Why am I like this?

Yuantong asked: "Although this is the Way of becoming Buddha, I'm reluctant to discard the gate of karma. Can you explain why I'm like this?"

Wansong replied: "On the contrary, one skewer pierces through."

Linquan's Verse

On the contrary, one skewer pierces through
Many drop the search
Subtle, subtle thinking
Sincerely, sincerely discerning transcendence
Conjecture!
The jackdaw is exactly black; the crane is exactly white

Commentary

"Why am I like this? Why, oh, why?"

It's right there. "Why?" is it. "Why?" is holding back, declining to pierce through with one skewer.

Linquan is as correct for today as he was for the 13th century northern China. Many drop the search and pretend to be satisfied with faith, thinking, and dualistically reasoning through life and the Buddha Way.

An oh-so-sincere, sincere discernment with subtle subtlety in the search for subtle, subtle thinking to justify their transcendence.

Conjecture that obscures the simple and direct truth:

Today, Lake Superior near the Neyaashi Zen Hermitage is deep dark blue. The morning mist is misty white.

31

Why do Buddhas tend to be palace-born?

Yuantong asked: "'All the buddhas do not appear in the world.' Then why do they tend to be palace-born?"

Wansong replied: "The green mountains are always walking."[73]

Linquan's Verse

The green mountains are always walking
All five eyes[74] should gaze at the problem
Not hiding the great circle
Because it is not the same as the conventional,
it is the same as the conventional
The warp and weft is desire and no desire

Commentary

This question begins with what appears to be a quote from Yuanwu's commentary to *The Blue Cliff Record*, Case 23, although it could appear in other places in dharma literature as well. Here it is:

All the buddhas do not appear in the world, nor is there a nirvana. Such things appear as skillful means to ferry beings across.[75]

The main idea is that buddha and nirvana are no buddhas and no nirvana. They exist in name only, like all things. These buddhas as well as the nirvana in which they non-abide, are just skillful means to benefit living beings, who likewise exist only like a "star at dawn, a bubble in a stream, a flash of lightning in a summer cloud, a flickering lamp, a phantom, and a dream."[76]

---

73 A statement of Furong Daokai. See Eihei Dogen, *Treasury of the True Dharma Eye: Zen Master Dogen's Shobo Genzo*, "Mountains and Waters Sutra," trans., Kazuaki Tanahashi (Boston: Shambhala Publications, 2010), 154.

74 Five eyes: fleshly eye, divine eye, wisdom eye, dharma eye, buddha eye.

75 Yuanwu Keqin, *The Blue Cliff Record*, Case 23, trans., Dosho Port (unpublished).

76 This popular version of the *Diamond Sutra's* last verse is attributed to A.F. Price.

Yuantong then waggishly asks, if they don't really exist, how come, as in the story of Shakyamuni Buddha, they always have upper-class births, in palaces even? Where are the working-class Buddhas? The Buddhas of the bowery?

Shakyamuni Buddha, though, was actually born under a flowering sala tree that had leaned down such that Queen Maya could grasp onto it for support during her labor. Queen Maya was on the way from her husband's palace to her parents' palace, so close enough for Zen work – let's not get tangled in buddhology.

Wansong leaps through the question and the quibbling, quoting the great Caodong master, Furong Daokai, "The green mountains are always walking." Palace-born buddhas do not appear in the world – what's that got to do with green mountains walking?

Our Zen Way invites us to be free from limited perspectives. One system that calls for freedom through practice is the five eyes – the human eye, the heavenly eye, the wisdom eye, the dharma eye, and the buddha eye. The human eye is ordinary seeing the self, others, and things of the world as separate and enduring. The heavenly eye sees self, others, and things of the world from the perspective of steady states of absorption (aka, samadhi), characterized by bliss and expansiveness. The wisdom eye sees the nonduality and emptiness of the self, others, and things of the world, smashing to bits any separation and self-existence. The dharma eye sees all things as skillful means to benefit the suffering the self, others, and things of the world. And the buddha eye sees through all the first four lenses at once.

In *The Diamond Sutra,* Chapter 18, just after the Buddha has explained to Subhuti the emptiness of *all* dharmas, including his own awakening, he takes up the five eyes to give five perspectives on this one world. As Linquan puts it in verse, "All five eyes should gaze at the problem/Not hiding the great circle."

Buddha and all of his eyes did not appear in the world. The deep blue lake is always swimming.

in Mu Soeng, *The Diamond Sutra: Transforming the Way We Perceive the World* (Somerville, MA: Wisdom Publications, 2000), 61.

32

Why do extinction
between the twin sala trees?

Yuantong asked: "Also, there is no nirvana. Then, why do extinction between the twin sala trees?"

Wansong replied: "In bright light, not turning the wheel."

Linquan's Verse

> In bright light, not turning the wheel
> Hidden, going through spring outside kalpas
> Do not crave discursive investigation from dawn to dusk
> Obscuring the original person, the original person
> In the field of touch, be the object, the undefiled object

Commentary

This question, answer, and verse completes the previous question, answer, and verse, continuing the twinning format of *Going Through the Mystery's One Hundred Questions.*

The question here addresses the second part of the quote from Yuanwu, "nor is there any nirvana:"

> All the buddhas do not appear in the world, nor is there
> a nirvana. Such things appear as skillful means to ferry
> beings across.[77]

After arousing the Way Seeking Mind, determined to liberate all beings, our first task on the bodhisattva path is to realize the emptiness of the self. The second is to realize the emptiness of dharmas, the things of the world, including the buddhadharma. Yes, we apply the insight into emptiness to all aspects of this strange religion, including the emptiness of buddhas and nirvana.

Yuantong's tongue-in-cheek questions begin with the noble birth of buddhas and ends with their death between two sala trees. Sala trees (*shorea robusta*) play a large role in the buddhadharma, beyond their being

---

77   Yuanwu Keqin, *The Blue Cliff Record*, Case 23, trans., Dosho Port (unpublished).

the site of Shakyamuni Buddha's birth and death. Growing to a towering 130 feet tall, they flower very briefly and so became a symbol of the beauty and majesty of this fleeting world. When the Buddha was born, as mentioned in the previous chapter, a flowering sala tree bent down so that his mother, Queen Maya, could grasp a branch while giving birth. At the end of Shakyamuni's 80 years, he laid down between two sala trees, and when he died, the trees flowered out of season, and their petals rained down on his body. Their trunks then turned white.

Yuantong's question, though, is without adornment. If buddhas are not born, then how is it that they, or at least Shakyamuni, died between two sala trees? So as not to throw shade on the buddhadharma, buddhas turn the wheel in the dark, in the spring outside of kalpas, that is, in a flowering place beyond time.

When we just wag our mouths in the bright light, following the curiosities of our discursive intellect, we obscure just this person, the One Person, the original person (repeated in the verse just in case you missed it).

Linquan ends his verse with another version of the essential, liberating practice instruction, couched in a different context, that he's offered before (and will again):

In the field of touch, be the object, the undefiled object.

33

What is the essence of mind?

Yuantong asked: "Bodhidharma came from the west, 'not established on words or texts.' So why the diamond-hard saying, "*Lanka* is the essence of my mind?'"

Wansong replied: "Reliance is exactly the essence of mind."

Linquan's Verse

Reliance is exactly the essence of mind
Exterminating the profound mystery
Suddenly penetrate the Zen gateway
Pass through heaven's single opening
Unexpectedly, the old, blue-eyed foreign monk
provokes his attendant's laughter – and he's still laughing!

Commentary

In this question, Yuantong raises a couple phrases attributed to Bodhidharma. The first is from a famous verse, considered the summation of his teaching and of Zen itself. Here is a raw, character-by-character rendering:

Separate transmission outside teaching
Not established words, texts
Point directly human heart
See nature become buddha[78]

Yuantong quotes the second line of verse, 不立文字, not established (or relying or standing) on words or texts. I'll return to a consideration of this verse in "Question 80: Disclosing Zen insight."

And, yet, the ancestor also is reputed to have said, "*Lanka* is the essence of my mind." *Lanka* is the nickname for *The Lankavatara Sutra*, an important text in both ancient India and East Asia that emphasizes practice, the mind-only perspective, the storehouse consciousness, and buddhanature. It is clearly a contradiction to say, on the one hand, that

---

78 Trans., Dosho Port (unpublished).

the essence of mind is outside sutras and not to rely on words and texts, and then say that words from a text are the essence of mind.

In Western Zen, the former statement is given much more attention than the latter. This, however, is not the case in the Soto lineage of Katagiri Roshi where study is one of the three "legs" of training, along with zazen and engagement. And Wansong, in *The Record of Going Easy*, lays out the foci like this:

> To depend on understanding the sutras is to wrong the Buddhas of the three worlds. Parting from one letter of the sutras is the same as reverting to magic spells.[79]

In response to Yuantong's question, Wansong stresses the correct or true essence of mind. What is that? The profound mystery must be wiped out by passing through the Zen gateway. The essence of mind is never apart from you right where you are. Then why don't we notice?

Tsoknyi Rinpoche in the Dzogchen tradition jokes it out this way:

> You might jokingly tell *rigpa* [the essence of mind], "Hey, you were here all the time! I've been looking and looking for you all over the place. I spent so much money trying to find you, buying all these airplane tickets and flying here and there, doing all this searching. And you've been right here all the while! What's the matter with you?"

And rigpa might reply,

> I didn't go anywhere, and I wasn't trying to hide from you either. You can blame me, but I'm not really to blame. What am I supposed to do if you are always so busy searching elsewhere? I was always with you. From the moment you were born, from the very beginning, I've been right here with you. You just didn't notice. You were always preoccupied, paying attention to something else.[80]

Speaking of jokes, Bodhidharma, the old blue-eyed snaggle-toothed foreigner, told a real zinger alright – don't rely on words because they cover the essence of mind and here's some words that are the essence. Get it?

---

79 Wansong Xingxiu, *The Record of Going Easy*, Case 58: *The Diamond Sutra's Disparagement*, trans., Dosho Port. (unpublished).

80 Tsoknyi Rinpoche, *Fearless Simplicity: The Dzogchen Way of Living Simply in a Complex World* (Hong Kong: Rangjung Yeshe Publications, 2003), 129-130.

The attendant that Linquan refers to in his verse might be Huike, the second ancestor, or it might be you.

The essence of mind is still just laughing timelessly.

34

Why did Bodhidharma say, "I've pacified your mind?"

Yuantong asked: "The second ancestor searched for mind, but couldn't grasp it. Why say, 'I'm harmonizing my mind. It is not about you.'"

Wansong replied: "'Do not concern yourself with it.'"

Linquan's Verse

Do not concern yourself with it
The elder seems to cut the length, depending on
    repairing the fault
Moving through the sky, the Three Stars Mansion is the
    root of no-form
Why toil for a special, unusual life?

Commentary

This question continues what we started in "Question 29: What is Bodhidharma's usefulness?

The second ancestor, Huike, famously came to Bodhidharma's cave above the Shaolin Monastery and beseeched the old sage to admit him as a student. Even though night was upon them and it was beginning to snow, Bodhidharma ignored him. At dawn, with snow up to his waist, Huike took out a knife and cut off his arm. This got the old monk's attention, and after some emergency first-aid, I hope, he began his face-to-face work with Huike. Notably, other sources say that Huike lost his arm in an incident with bandits. So maybe he gave up what he didn't have in the first place.

The whole brutal drama with a very happy ending is recorded in *The No Gate Barrier*:

> Bodhidharma sat facing the wall. The second ancestor stood in the snow, cut off his arm, and said, "Your disciple's mind is not yet calm. I beg the teacher to pacify mind." Bodhidharma said, "Invite mind to arrive. I'll give you calm." The second ancestor said, "I have sought

mind, but cannot grasp it." Bodhidharma said, "Indeed, your mind has been pacified."[81]

After receiving the mind seal, Huike taught for thirty years. I'll let Keizan tell the next part of the story:

> After this entrustment, he preached the dharma as needed in [the capitol]. The fourfold assembly took refuge in him. In this manner, thirty years piled up, hiding his light and covering his tracks, and changing his deportment. Sometimes he entered taverns or passed through the doorways of butchers, and sometimes he conversed with people in the marketplace or followed along with lowly laborers. Once a person questioned him, saying, "Master, you are a person of the Way. Why do you behave in this manner?" The Master [Huike] said, "I am regulating my own mind. What concern is it of yours?"[82]

These last couple sentences, I've translated as 'I'm harmonizing my mind. It is not about you.'" Yuantong, given his wonderful oppositional nature, something I can relate to, noticed the rub between searching for mind and not being able to grasp it *and* Huike's later practice of harmonizing "my" mind.

In other words, Yuantong is asking, what's all this about "my" "mind"? Isn't the dharma about giving up on the "I," "me," "my?" And how could one person, even the great sage, harmonize what is neither personal nor graspable?

"It is not about you?" is the first part of a colloquial expression. Wansong fills in the rest: "Do not concern yourself with it." When all things are at rest, there is no need for concern.

It's early evening now in the Neyaashi Zen Hermitage. Tetsugan Sensei is on the other side of the state, attending to a friend who's having surgery in the morning. It's been windy and rainy all day as I settle into a several-day solo retreat. The storm windows rattle and the first snow of the season falls so evenly all around.

The next line of verse, "The elder seems to cut the length, depending on repairing the fault," refers to Bodhidharma, the elder, and likens his student to a flute, who actually may have cut his own arm, just as a

---

81 Wumen Huikai, *The No Gate Barrier*, Case 41: Bodhidharma Pacifies Mind, in trans., Dosho Port (unpublished).

82 Keizan Jokin, *Record of the Transmission of Illumination*, Volume 1, trans., William M. Bodiford (Tokyo: Soto shu Shumucho, 2017), 262-263.

bamboo flute maker will take a long section of bamboo and cut away the part not needed.

"Moving through the sky, the Three Stars Mansion is the root of no-form." "The Three Stars Mansion" is Orion in the Western nomenclature for constellations. The whole night sky seems to rotate around it. Remarkable and ungraspable as a single snowflake falling.

"Why toil for a special, unusual life?"

35

How to investigate?

Yuantong asked: "*The Prajna[paramita Sutras* speak of twenty emptinesses. How to pick and choose?"

Wansong replied: "Not many; not few."

Linquan's Verse

Not many; not few
Perfectly clear, perfectly clear
The third ancestor's words
Make it explicit for you
The ultimate truth is not difficult – an intimate line of
    verse
Great compassion makes difficult trouble for Mara

Commentary

The Prajnaparamita Sutras, the title of several sutras of varying length and a name for a category of sutras, enumerate lists with a number of numbers for types of emptiness. Wait, emptiness has types? you might reasonably ask.

All phenomena, of course, are empty and so the list could be pretty big. Nevertheless, one of the lists includes twenty emptinesses: the emptiness of subject; object; subject and object; the emptiness of emptiness; great emptiness; of ultimate reality; of the conditioned; of the unconditioned; of the infinite; of the beginningless and endless; of nonrepudiation; of essential nature; of all dharmas; of own-marks; of unascertainable; of nonexistence of own-mark; of existence; of nonexistence; of own-being; of other-being.[83]

Yuantong's question here seems to be referring to the *Faith in Mind* poem by the third ancestor in China, Sengcan (died 606), because he borrows "picking and choosing" (唯嫌揀擇) from his line, "The Great Way is without difficulty, it only dislikes picking and choosing." How to pick and choose (揀擇) an emptiness? You gotta love this waggish guy.

Wansong responds, "Not many, not few," opening a whole new

---

83 For a detailed explanation of each of the twenty emprinesses, see *The Large Sutra on Perfect Wisdom: With the Divisions of the Abhisamayalankara*, trans., Edward Conze (Berkeley: University of California Press, 1975), 144-148.

panorama of emptinesses.

That might have been a good place to leave it. But Linquan gets Yuantong's "picking and choosing" playfulness, so quotes the leading line from a poem, "The Great Way is without difficulty," while appreciating the radical intimacy of this path of falling down and getting up.

These three practitioners of old are all smeared with mud. When skillfully giving the self to the self, and others to others, where is the seam for a picking-and-choosing Mara to get a word in edgewise?

36

Are they the same or different?

Yuantong asked: "*The Diamond Sutra's* four characteristics. *The Complete Enlightenment Sutra's* four characteristics. Are they the same or different?"

Wansong replied: "Different tethers – no moxibustion for this illness."

Linquan's Verse

Different tethers – no moxibustion for this illness
Old Lu gathered authority
Seizing the vertical at the last moment
You see the nature of life
Iron-ride Zen harmonizes with not needing to strive
Intimately returning, the four oceans are clear as a mirror

Commentary

Yuantong not only knew his Zen lineage, but he also had a deep intimacy with the sutras. The four characteristics that *The Diamond Sutra* and *The Sutra of Complete Enlightenment* have in common are the four ideas of personhood (我人四相): a self; a person; a living being; and a life force. *The Diamond Sutra* returns to these four marks frequently, while *The Sutra of Complete Enlightenment* works through them once in the chapter, "Bodhisattva Cleansed of All Karmic Obstruction."[84]

The first characteristic, "self," refers to the idea that the self comprises the aggregates of form, feeling, perceptions, formations, or the consciousness aggregate that perceives them. The second characteristic, "person," refers to the sense that this set of aggregates is distinct from other sets, so it is the mark of "I" and "thou." The third characteristic, "living being," is the stage of appreciating that all living beings are together in that they consist of five aggregates. And the fourth characteristic, "life force," is that which remains when the three stages of a self, a person, and a living being melt away.

Although there is progression from the focus on the self, to a more

---

84   *The Sutra of Complete Enlightenment*, trans., Guo-gu (Elmhurst, NY: Dharma Drum Publications, 1997), 50-55.

expansive sense of being, to appreciating the sameness of living beings, these are all just frames, perspectives. The life force too is still a perspective that must also melt away in the pot of boiling practice in order to be thoroughly cleansed of all karmic obstruction.

Just as Yuantong has demonstrated his subtle understanding of koans in the previous chapters, here we see his sensitive sutra-comparing mind. However, Wansong doesn't take the well-thought-through bait coming from Yuantong's human eye. Every system is a skillful means to set us free. When we attach to it and to our human eye's thinking about it (comparing, contrasting, believing, doubting), it becomes an incurable disease. Close, close! Accord with the buddhadharma.

Fortunately, old Lu, that is, the sixth ancestor, Huineng, got the gist, the inner meaning of *The Diamond Sutra*, first glimpsing his self-nature when he heard a monk chanting in the marketplace, "Abiding nowhere, let the mind come forth." Had he heard it as an object of perception, the dharma would not have been transmitted through him to us. Instead, Huineng became abiding nowhere and the mind came forth.

Linquan's "Seizing the vertical at the last moment," may refer to Huineng receiving dharma transmission from the fifth ancestor, Hongren, late at night (at the last moment), then crossing the river and practicing diligently in the mountains for ten years.

The rigors of diligent practice, so-called "iron-ride Zen," harmonize with fully and completely letting go.

Intimately returning, the four oceans are clear as a mirror.

37

Which method is most intimate?

Yuantong asked: "Of the *Surangama Sutra's* twenty-five kinds of complete going through, which one is most intimate?"

Wansong replied: "A good guest does not neglect their companion."

Linquan's Verse

> A good guest does not neglect their companion
> It isn't necessary to repeatedly judge
> South Mountain shares North Mountain
> Imposing manner polishes a person
> A dark cloud supports the bright moon
> Many people are divided by love and hate
> Accept the division of beautiful or ugly
> I say, use one to pierce through

Commentary

What's the best way to awaken?

You, dear reader, might be looking for the best way. If so, this question invites extensive excavation.

The Surangama Sutra focuses on the spiritual journey. Indeed, "Surangama" could be rendered "heroic march," and as such has long been a particularly important teaching for those on the Zen path. Here is Charles Luk summarizing one of the important passages in the sutra:

> The Buddha orders the twenty-five enlightened ones in the assembly to disclose the various means by which they have attained enlightenment so that others can learn something from them. After their statements of their realization by means of the six sense data, six sense organs, six consciousnesses and seven elements of fire, earth, water, wind, space, consciousness and perception, the World Honoured One asks Manjushri for his

opinion on these twenty-five methods."[85]

Just as Buddha asked Manjushri, Yuantong asks Wansong, of the twenty-five gates of entry, which is the most intimate for what's called consummate interpenetration or complete going through.

Before we get to the issue of which one is most intimate, though, let me give you a smell, a taste, and a touch of the twenty-five methods.

First, the experience of Sublimity of Fragrance:

> I observed that when monks lit sandalwood incense, its fragrance silently entered my nostrils. In contemplation I realized that the source of fragrance was neither wood, nor space, nor smoke, nor fire; it came from no place and went to no place. As a result of this contemplation, my distinction-making consciousness disappeared, and I gained freedom from outflows.... Fragrance as I had perceived it vanished, but its wondrousness, which had been hidden, was everywhere revealed to me. So it was that I became an Arhat through contemplating the sublimity within fragrance.[86]

Second, a pair of doctors, twins, who had tasted 108,000 kinds of herbal medicine, then they began studying with the Buddha:

> While reverently serving the Buddha, we came to understand that the nature of flavors is that they are neither empty nor existent. We understood that flavors do not arise from the body nor from the mind, nor are they independent of the body and mind. Thus by discerning the differences among flavors, we became enlightened.[87]

And third and best-known also occurs as a koan in *The Blue Cliff Record.* Sixteen bodhisattvas had simultaneous kenshos while taking a bath, just as they touched the water.[88] One of the sixteen speaks for the group:

---

85 *The Surangama Sutra*, trans., Charles Luk, http://www.buddhanet.net/pdf_file/surangama.pdf, 19.

86 *The Surangama Sutra – A New Translation with Excerpts from the Commentary by the Venerable Master Hsuan Hua*, trans., Surangama Sutra Translation Committee of the Buddhist text Translation Society (Ukiah: Buddhist Text Translation Society, 2017), 207-209. Modified.

87 Ibid., 209. Modified.

88 Yuanwu Keqin, *The Blue Cliff Record*, Case 78, trans., Dosho Port: "In the old days there were sixteen bodhisattvas. When they entered the bath at the appointed time

When it was time to bathe, I followed the custom and entered the bathhouse. Suddenly, upon contact with the water, I understood that the water was neither washing away the dirt nor washing my body. In the midst of this I became tranquil as I understood that there was nothing there."[89]

The sutra includes examples of individuals and groups who gained entry into nonduality through twenty-two more dharma doors, and their opinion, based on their personal experience, about which is the best door. This section of the sutra concludes with the testimony of Avalokiteshvara, the Bodhisattva of Compassion, who hears the cries of the world. Spoiler alert: the sutras often save the best for last. Avalokiteshvara's report, however, is too long to share in full, so I will excerpt just a short passage, referring you to *The Surangama Sutra* itself for further study:

First I redirected my hearing inward in order to enter the current of the sages. Then external sounds disappeared. With the direction of my hearing reversed and with sounds stilled, both sounds and silence ceased to arise. So it was that, as I gradually progressed, what I heard and my awareness of what I heard came to an end. Even when that state of mind in which everything had come to an end disappeared, I did not rest. My awareness and the objects of my awareness were emptied, and when that process of emptying my awareness was wholly complete, then even that emptying and what had been emptied vanished. Coming into being and ceasing to be themselves ceased to be. Then the ultimate stillness was revealed. All of a sudden I transcended the worlds of ordinary beings, and I also transcended the worlds of beings who have transcended the ordinary worlds. Everything in the ten directions was fully illuminated....[90]

What are the takeaways from this vast and rolling discourse?

First, awakening is common and accessible through our normal

---

according to the rule, all of them realized the cause of water. Worthies, how do you see their saying, 'Subtle touch gives forth light; we have achieved the state of Buddha's offspring.' You must go through seven and enter eight – only then will you get it."

89 Op Cit., *The Surangama Sutra – A New Translation with Excerpts from the Commentary by the Venerable Master Hsuan Hua*, 208. Modified.

90 Ibid., 235-236.

human sense experience. Second, there are innumerable ways to awaken and the doors are always with us, just as we are, just what we are – seeing, hearing, tasting, touching, smelling, and thinking. And third, all the great practitioners in the sutra thought that the door they entered through was the best, so be wary of any teacher who insists that their way is the only way. It may well be that the door they stress was best for them, of course, but what about you?

Fortunately, Buddha had Manjusri, the Bodhisattva of Nondual Wisdom, standing by to discern just this very point. And so the Buddha said,

> In fact, none of the methods employed by these sages can be ranked as superior or inferior to the others. But now it is Ananda whom I wish to teach how to become enlightened. Which of these twenty-five methods of practice is most suitable for beings at Ananda's level? And which one, after my nirvana, will lead beings of this world to practice in accord with the Vehicle of the Bodhisattvas and to follow the path to supreme enlightenment? Which of these methods will lead them most easily to success?[91]

In other words, which method would be most fitting for Ananda, which would be most fitting for those with a Bodhisattva predisposition, and which is easiest? Manjushri, at considerable length including verse, praises the Avalokiteshvara's meditation on hearing, and says that the meditation described by Avalokiteshvara would be best for Ananda and Bodhisattva aspirants in the future.

Wansong cuts through the sutra's wonderful erudition with the simple truth: "A good guest does not neglect their companion."

Or as Stephen Stills put it, "If you can't be with the one you love, love the one you're with."

Yes, this isn't a contest. It's not really about the preferences of the identity center. Use this very gate for an entrance. The different methods are different in name only – "South Mountain shares North Mountain." Undertake the training with vigor and dignity. Our limitations show us our clarity, our shadows punctuate our brightness. Without justifying the lack of diligent practice or resorting to a phony cognitive reframe, turn the light around, illuminate the source of seeing, hearing, tasting, touching, smelling, or thinking.

I say, use one to pierce through.

---

91 Ibid., 248.

38

What is the highest place?

Yuantong asked: "'Step-by-step scale the heights of transformation.' What is the highest place?"

Wansong replied: "The bottom of the great ocean."

Linquan's Verse

> The bottom of the great ocean
> Why did the ancestors gather an assembly?
> Just to be present on the separate peak
> Undeniably, partially-cooked rice

Commentary

Surprisingly, in this question, Yuantong quotes a capping phrase by Wansong, "Step-by-step scale the heights of transformation"[92] that appears in *The Record of Going Easy*. The highest place, the ultimate point of transformation, the peak of wonder, where is it?

The ancestors set up teaching halls just for this reason. Look around! Snakes and dragons entangled. The very top is the very bottom. The very bottom is the very top. Is that person struggling through the first period of zazen in a seven-day sesshin the very top or the very bottom?

Step-by-step, the peak of wonder.

This morning, just before sunrise, we headed to the lake. Snow had fallen during the night and a pure, trackless snow covered the earth – except for coyote and fox tracks dodging from the undergrowth onto the human path. The coyote and fox went the same way, so no knowing which was following the other. Then they turned back into the undergrowth, although the fox went west toward the city, and the coyote turned east toward the forest-covered point.

Half-cooked rice is perfectly and completely half-cooked.

---

92 Wansong Xingxiu, *The Record of Going Easy*, Case 28: Huguo's Three Embarrassments, trans., Dosho Port. (unpublished).

39

How does a person lay it all down?

Yuantong asked: "'It is difficult to lay down thought after thought.' How does a person lay it all down?"

Wansong replied: "Carry it along."

Linquan's Verse

Carry it along
Zhaozhou's most intimate place
Holding a full alms bowl, a single thing comes, no?
Do not follow the arising of egotistical anxiety

Commentary

How is it when up is down (as in the last chapter) and letting it all go is carrying it all along? Thomas Cleary notes that these two phrases put together comprise a common Zen expression. His translation: "Climbing higher with every step is easy; putting down every state of mind is hard."[93]

Yuantong takes this and raises an issue that also quotes from Wansong's capping phrases for a koan in his book, *The Record of Going Easy*, Huguo's Three Embarrassments, as in the last chapter. Here he raises the same issue in slightly different form as Yanyang in "Case 57: Yanyang's Single Thing."

First for Case 57:

> Yanyang Sonja asked Zhaozhou, "When not a single thing comes, how is it?'"
> Zhou said, "Put it down." Yan said, "When not a single thing comes, how do you put it down?" Zhou said, "If so, carry it along."[94]

Wansong gives the same answer to Yuantong's question as Zhaozhou in Case 57: How can I let go of thought after thought? "Carry it along."

---

93 Thomas Cleary, *One Hundred Questions: A Chan Buddhist Classic*, Kindle Edition, 42.

94 Wansong Xingxiu, *The Record of Going Easy*, Case 57: Yanyang Single Thing, trans., Dosho Port (unpublished).

How is carrying it along, letting go of it all?
Put it down.

This might seem like word play but look again – this is Wansong's (and Zhaozhou's) most intimate place. Linquan joins the warp and woof fun of it all, embedding another Zhaozhou koan in his verse, "Zhaozhou's Wash the Bowl:"

> A monk asked Zhaozhou, "I have just entered the monastery. Please, teacher, give me instruction." Zhaozhou asked, "Have you eaten your gruel yet?" The monk said, "Yes, I have." Zhaozhou said, "Go wash your bowl."[95]

Going Through the Mystery's One Hundred Questions contains an intensity of weaving and interlocking narratives that is quite extraordinary!

The third line of Linquan's verse is "Holding a full alms bowl, a single thing comes, no?" This splices the thread from "Zhaozhou's Wash the Bowl," with reference to the alms bowl and "Huguo's Three Embarrassments" with reference to a single thing. However, in the bowl koan, the monk reports that he has eaten; and in the embarrassment koan "not a single thing arrives," while in Linquan's verse, a single thing does arrive.

"A single thing," 一物, in the Zen lexicon, is thusness. The luminous One Mind. When we let go of the arrival of egotistical anxiety, coming and not, letting go and carrying on, the bowl is empty or the bowl is full, amazingly, we are all just the arrival of the single thing.

---

95 Wumen Huikai, *The No Gate Barrier*, Case 7: Zhaozhou's Wash the Bowl, trans., Dosho Port (unpublished).

40

Who can escape Yangqi's diamond trap?

Yuantong asked: "Who can escape Yangqi's diamond trap?"

Wansong replied: "Passed through."

Linquan's Verse

Passed through
This great barrier, twisting around the heavens
Lightning and flint sparks move slowly
Inevitably, they intimately see through

Commentary

Yangqi Fanghui (Japanese, Yogi; 995-1049) was an important teacher in the Linji succession. As a young man, he was a tax collector, but got into trouble with his higher-ups, and so had to flee into obscurity. What better way to hide than become a monk? This obscurity didn't last, however, and he became the monastery director under Shishuang Chuyuan (also known as Ciming, 986-1039). Yangqi repeatedly asked him about the essence of the buddhadharma, and Shishuang repeatedly told him, "You are the temple director. Please take care of temple affairs."[96]

After knocking his teacher into the mud, Yangqi finally got the message and realized great awakening. He founded a line of teachers that continued through Hakuin in Japan and still continues today in China, Korea, Japan, and the West. Yangqi's diamond trap is usually paired with a chestnut burr. We'll deal with the chestnut in the next chapter.

Yangqi's diamond trap and chestnut burr is a teaching device to help people wake up. The "diamond" here, 金剛, could also be rendered "vajra" or "adamantine." And "trap," 圈, could also be "ring" or "pitfall." The main idea is that you find yourself in an incredibly difficult jam, a diamond trap, twisting and turning through the heavens, even. How could you get free?

The Cautionary Instructions for the Dark Gate, a Chan text from the

---

96 For more details see Andy Ferguson, *Zen's Chinese Heritage: The Masters and Their Teachings* (Boston: Wisdom, 2000), 377. Or for a more colorful retelling, see Xutang Zihu, *Record of Empty Hall: One Hundred Classic Koans*, trans., Dosho Port (Boulder: Shambhala Publications, 2021), 177-178.

fourteenth century, written by a Yangqi lineage monk named Yongzhong, has this promise for those who pass through the diamond trap, who swallow the chestnut burr:

> In the Yangqi transmission, we use the diamond trap and chestnut burr to test mistaken and correct. You can pass through the Iron Mountain Enclosure, but not the diamond trap. You can swallow the great ocean, but not a chestnut burr. If you swallow one burr, you can swallow one hundred, ten million, one hundred million burrs without obstruction. If you can pass through the diamond trap, you can pass through one hundred, ten million, one hundred million.[97]

Maybe you can escape the Iron Mountain Enclosure that in ancient Indian cosmology surrounds the human world, or swallow the great ocean with some miraculous tricks or psychedelic trips. But even supernormal powers cannot free one from the diamond trap that makes flashes of lightning and sparks from a flintstone appear to move slowly.

The last line of Linguan's verse is like comfort food after a tough sesshin: "Inevitably, they intimately see through."

A good dharma friend might say, "It's okay, really, it's okay. Put your head on my shoulder and cry for a while."

Inevitably. Sounds like it might be a while.

How to be free of the diamond trap?

---

97 緇門警訓 Zimen jingxun; Japanese, Shimon kyokun; Korean, Ch'imun kyonghun. https://21dzk.l.u-tokyo.ac.jp/SAT2018/T2023.html, trans., Dosho Port (unpublished).

41

Who can swallow
Yangqi's chestnut burr?

Yuantong asked: "Who can swallow Yangqi's chestnut
burr?"

Wansong replied: "Done."

Linquan's Verse

Done
Marvelous function, spiritual power – not a small thing![98]
Replace the lantern in the Buddha Hall with one that
    looks just like it
Now, don't judge who is shining

Commentary

"Who can swallow Yangqi's chestnut burr?"
    A wonderful koan!
    This is the second of Yangqi's two barriers, the first was addressed in
the previous chapter. A chestnut burr is covered with nasty thorns that

---

98   "Marvelous function, spiritual power" is probably a reference to Layman Pang:

One day Shih-T'ou said to the Layman: "Since seeing me, what have your
daily activities been?" "When you ask me about my daily activities, I can't
open my mouth," the Layman replied. "Just because I know you are thus I
now ask you," said Shih-t'ou. Whereupon the Layman offered this verse:

My daily activities are not unusual,
I'm just naturally in harmony with them.
Grasping nothing, discarding nothing,
In every place there's no hindrance, no conflict.
Who assigns the ranks of vermilion and purple?
The hills' and mountains' last speck of dust
is extinguished.
[My] supernatural power and marvelous activity—
Drawing water and carrying firewood.

From *The Recorded Sayings of Layman P'ang*, trans., Ruth Fuller, (New York:
Weatherhill, 1971), 46.

jut out from the casing of the nut. And you think this moment is hard to swallow? Come on! How would you approach the issue of swallowing a chestnut burr?

Well, first off, any "approach" and you're in the world of "me" and "it" and you ain't gonna do it. It's like the hot iron ball that Wumen presents in his commentary on the mu koan (although the diamond trap and chestnut burr are usually used in the tradition to refer to post-kensho training). Nevertheless:

> Do not do it as nothingness. Do not do it as have or have not. As if you've swallowed a hot iron ball – vomit and vomit but it won't go out. Wash away your former harmful knowledge and harmful feelings. Be skillful for a long, long time. Naturally, you'll succeed, breaking inside and outside. One day, you will be a mute person dreaming. Just allow self-knowledge.[99]

As you explore this issue through the body, I wish you smooth passage.

Meanwhile, Wansong, fully replete with self-knowledge, is already smacking his lips and reaching for another chestnut burr, for one hundred, ten million, one hundred million.

A side issue here is that Wansong, a Caodong lineage monk, is tested with a question about how a monk in the Linji-Yangqi lineage might express freedom. It seems that in the old days, generally speaking, as I've been saying here repeatedly, there wasn't as much difference between lineages as there is today. Ah, those were the days, my friend. Some teachers in the present Zen community seem to view the essence of Zen to be different among the different lineages. They might find this very point, indeed, hard to swallow.

So let's move on to the verse.

Linquan recognizes "marvelous function, spiritual power" when he sees them. "Marvelous function," 妙用, is a common term for a Zen master's activity to skillfully use whatever is at hand in the service of liberation. "Spiritual power," 神通, could also be translated "supernormal cognition," referring to great enlightenment in the service of the many beings.

In the third line of Linquan's verse, he refers to a koan involving the great Yunmen, so a third Zen lineage joins the choir, all singing the same tune. "Replace the lantern in the Buddha Hall with one that looks just like it."

Yunmen addressed the assembly saying,

---

99 Wumen Huikai, *The No Gate Barrier*, Case 1: Zhaozhou's Dog, trans., Dosho Port. (unpublished).

> Within Heaven and Earth, amidst the reaches of infinite
> time, there is a jewel hidden in the mountain of form.
> Take a lantern and go to the Buddha hall. Bring the
> triple gate and put it on the lantern.[100]

The triple gate, by the way, is the main monastery gate with a room on the top with all the bodhisattvas and arhats arranged along each side – not a small thing! Marvelous function! Spiritual power! Turns out it was hidden right here in this stinking human form.

Linquan shows his marvelous function by noting that if you succeed in replacing the lamp in the Buddha Hall, it'll look just like the one that was hanging there before. This is a key point to illuminate.

Whatever you do, don't judge who is shining there wide awake – not a small thing!

---

100 Yuanwu Keqin, *The Blue Cliff Record*, Case 62, trans., Dosho Port (unpublished).

42

Have you gotten through?

Yuantong asked: "Have you gotten through Huanglong's Three Barriers?"

Wansong replied: "Only the Venerable."

Linquan's Verse

Only the Venerable
Unwilling to pass on one's responsibilities to others
A standard for 10,000 generations
The ten directions appear
The Buddha's hand, a donkey's leg!
Why use that to seek?
The karma of one's birth!
To answer requires turning toward the self

Commentary

Today, after morning zazen, I went down to the lake, as usual. It was about 30 degrees with a wind from the south at about 10 mph. As I went over the berm and down the path, I saw a small yellow and brown splotched dog standing at the transition point of the path to the beach. As I approached, he stood his ground. I'd seen this fella before and knew the woman who walked with him was probably coming up the beach. So I stopped, and the dog and I had a moment together making eye contact, neither of us advancing or retreating. As I'd been working on this chapter, and this question was on my mind, I said, "Hey, good dog, have you gotten through?"

Huanglong Huinan (Japanese, Oryo Enan; 1002-1069) was the founder of the Huanglong branch of the Linji lineage. Like Yangqi whose teaching was the subject of investigation in Questions 40 and 41, his life wasn't just sweet rice and sesame tofu. Huanglong became a monk at a young age, studied under numerous masters, and finally met Shishuang Chuyuan. He realized great awakening when he heard Shishuang present the "Zhaozhou Investigates an Old Woman" koan. There was no dog involved at all.

Shishuang was reputed to have had a wife who lived near the monastery, and whom he visited often. Yangqi's enlightenment occurred when Shishuang was returning to the monastery after one such visit, and Huanglong's awakening occurred with a koan about Zhaozhou making a visit to another old woman. Hmmm.

In any case, one of the first monasteries where Huanglong served as abbot caught fire and burned to the ground. Huanglong took full responsibility and served some time in prison before he was eventually pardoned. This appears to be eulogized by Linquan's verse lines, "Unwilling to pass on one's responsibilities to others/A standard for 10,000 generations."

After his pardon, Huanglong returned to teaching and trained several outstanding successors, including Huitang Zuxin (1025-1100) and Baofeng Kewen (1025-1102). Several generations later, his lineage was transmitted to Japan by Myoan Eisai (1141-1215). The Huanglong lineage eventually died out in China but continues today through the offspring of Eisai's second generation successor, Dogen – that is, through the Soto lineage.

Back to our present issue, our questioner, Yuantong, raised koans from the Yangqi line in the last two questions and here casually challenges Wansong with the quintessential teaching from the other main Linji line, Huanglong's Three Barriers. Huanglong's barriers continue to be worked today by students in the Harada-Yasutani koan curriculum, and also those Rinzai lines that work through *Entangling Vines*.

Here is how the case is framed in *Entangling Vines*:

> Huanglong always presented students with these three statements, but no one could come up with a satisfactory response. Monks everywhere called them the Huanglong's Three Barriers. Even with the few who gave answers, the master would neither agree nor disagree but only sit there in formal posture with eyes closed. No one could fathom his intent. When the layman Fan Yanzhi asked the reason for this, Huanglong replied, "Those who have passed through the gate shake their sleeves and go straight on their way. What do they care if there's a gatekeeper? Those who seek the gatekeeper's permission have yet to pass through."[101]

And here are the koans themselves:

> How is my hand like Buddha's hand?
> How is my leg like a donkey's leg?
> Everyone has a native place. Show me your native place.

101 *Entangling Vines: A Classic Collection of Zen Koans*, trans., Thomas Yuho Kirchner (Somerville, MA: Wisdom, 2013), 39. Modified.

How are you getting by with those then? Only a Venerable? Why use a Buddha's hand and a donkey's leg to seek awakening? The karma of your own birth, your native place, is the ten directions advancing. How could the answer to you be found somewhere other than the venerable you?

Certainly not in a yellow-brown splotched dog on the beach who, when asked, "Hey, good dog, have you gotten through?" just shook out his ears and trotted away.

43

Is this guest or host?

Yuantong asked: "Heh! HEH! Tell me, is this guest or is this host?"

Wansong replied: "Host and guest pass through thus."

Linquan's Verse

Now you're using a former example to demonstrate
A blind donkey extinguishes the treasury of the true
  dharma eye
Host and guest mutually participate, raising the
  opportunity
Intimate friends need not repeatedly reexamine a case

Commentary

First, let's look at the shouts. One shout and one deafening shout. This might be the Mahabodhi Monastery of Caodong master Wansong, but Yuantong is shouting it up like he was at Linji's place, or as Linquan notes unflatteringly without even quoting Wansong's response to start his verse, "Now you're using a former example to demonstrate:"

> The master [Linji] asked a monk, "Sometimes a shout is like the Diamond Sword of the Vajra King; sometimes a shout is like the golden-haired lion crouching on the ground; sometimes a shout is like a weed-tipped fishing pole; sometimes a shout doesn't function as a shout. How do you understand this?" The monk hesitated. The master gave a shout.[102]

Unlike Linji's one shout, Yuantong shouted, shouted again, and then asked Wansong if this was guest or host. He could be asking if his shouts demonstrated the relative or absolute, but given that he has been raising issues in relationship with the Linji lineage, he seems to be asking about Linji's Four Relationships of Host and Guest. In this system, the host can be seen as the teacher and the guest as the student. The four relationships

---

102 *The Record of Linji*, trans., Ruth Fuller Sasaki, edit. Thomas Yuho Kirchner (Honolulu: University of Hawai'i Press, 2009), 308.

are: guest examines the host; host examines the guest, host examines the host, guest examines the guest. Linji said,

> When host and guest meet they vie with each other in discussion. At times, in response to something, they may manifest a form; at times they may act with their whole body; or they may use tricks or devices to appear joyful or angry; or they may reveal half of the body; or again they may ride upon a lion or mount a lordly elephant.[103]

Is Yuantong's shout host or guest? Did it reveal the host or did it disclose the guest? In response, Wansong sings his own song, "Host and guest pass through thus," reframed by Linquan as "Host and guest mutually participate, raising the opportunity."

Inspiring! Yet, without entering the field of merit of one of these old worthies, how could we today see their marvelous function and spiritual powers? And what about the blind donkey? That is, the second line of verse, "A blind donkey extinguishes the treasury of the true dharma eye."

This is also a reference to Linji, specifically when he was about to die, or as Kirchner wonderfully renders the phrase, "reveals his nirvana":

> When the master [Linji] was about to pass away, he seated himself and said, "After I am extinguished, do not let my True Dharma Eye be extinguished." Sansheng came forward and said, "How could I let your True Dharma Eye be extinguished!" "Later on, when somebody asks you about it, what will you say to them?" asked the master. Sansheng gave a shout. "Who would have thought that my True Dharma Eye would be extinguished upon reaching this blind donkey!" said the master. Having spoken these words, sitting erect, the master revealed his nirvana.[104]

As in the above interaction, the mature teacher-student relationship might express itself like this – shouts and blind donkeys. Another phrase that's used in our Zen Way to express this kind of intimacy is "intimate friend," 知音. Literally, it could be translated as "knows the music."

See "Question 26: Who is able to hear it?" and "Question 60: Where is Enlightenment's exquisite flowering?" for other references to the intimate friend.

---

103 Ibid., 245.

104 Ibid., 340.

Your intimate friend knows your music, right?

The background story is that in an ancient text a master lute player had a friend who truly heard and understood their music. When the intimate friend died, the lute player gave up playing. This has come to represent the close teacher-student relationship where the student hears with the same ears as the teacher. Except that the student doesn't quit when the teacher dies, but finds a way to carry the tune.

And Yuantong isn't quite there. There's a clear sense in this question that Yuantong is playing Zen and not playing the same music as Wansong. As Linquan noticed, "Intimate friends need not repeatedly reexamine a case."

Just one shout would do nicely.

44

How about your understanding?

Yuantong, while holding the fly whisk erect, asked, "You have expounded Zen, but how is it for you?"

Wansong replied: "Today comfortably without attachments."

Linquan's Verse
Today comfortably without attachments
Very much seems like hiding soldiers and still losing a
    battle
The Tang Dynasty is broken and we're still seeking the
    problem
To go straight through, the only essential is a genuine
    teacher

Commentary

There is a surprising level of informal intimacy in these exchanges. In this case, similar to the last chapter where Yuantong used an informal form of "you" when raising his question, here he grabs Wansong's fly whisk. I imagine Yuantong and Wansong sitting in a beautiful room, doors open to a garden, face-to-face, with Linquan off to the side, taking notes, maybe cheering on the young upstart, smiling along with Wansong's responses.

Yuantong again challenges the old master – you can talk the talk, and you even convinced Genghis Khan that you were the real deal. But really how is it for you? Those of you fortunate enough to have been in, or perhaps continue to be in, such a relationship, have you ever asked your teacher this question?

I see old man Wansong here extending his arms, wrapping them around himself, and showing, this is it.

Linquan pushes the conversation further by raising the issue of losing a battle and yet having soldiers in reserve, just like the mystery of why the past was the way it was remains hidden to us. There are so many things we can't see or understand, like the clear presentation of the truth before our eyes, comfortably without attachments.

And maybe something is still hidden.

In the last line of the verse, Linquan tells us how we can know the dharma, "To go straight through, the only essential is a genuine teacher."

"Genuine teacher," 阿師 (Chinese and Japanese, ashi) by the way, is a term that is used interchangeably with "reliable master," 師家, (Chinese, shijia; Japanese, shike).

But don't make the mistake that many do on this path, over-relying on the genuine teacher, hiding behind their robes. Or fall on the other side of the path of misusing a teacher by denying that one is needed.

As for the "to go" and "straight through" parts of the message – those are for each one of us.

45

In one Revolution!

Yuantong, raising up a walking staff, asked: "In addition, there is twirling the head of the walking staff above and below, in one revolution, expressing the matter!"

Wansong replied: "Venerable elder."

Linquan's Verse

Elder – this beautiful word is sufficient to transcend
   passion
Motionless shield and spear establish great peace
The timely words of the purple swallow and the yellow
   oriole
Great sound is necessary for the silent fruition of faith

Commentary

Now the guy's got a hold of the walking staff! Twirling it this way and that. He's like a toddler and the old man hasn't child-proofed his meeting room. Lordy!

Wansong just calls out, "Venerable elder."

And I was just painting a picture with Wansong as the old sage, Linquan the middle-aged sage, and Yuantong, the young student. Erase that! It seems that Yuantong is an elder monk. And one source has Linquan's dates as 1223-1281, so if those are correct (which I doubt), he would have been less than twenty-three when Wansong died in 1246. In any case, there is reason to keep an open mind about just what is going on in these relationships.

Great peace is established without twirling a shield or a spear, let alone a walking staff. Great peace is all around and passing through, always right here, like the call of the birdies, the purple swallow and the yellow oriole. You don't need to do anything at all.

Great peace is the turning of the earth, sun, and moon. Last night was a near-total lunar eclipse. The forecast was for clouds, so I wasn't optimistic. But I got up a bit before 3:00am for a look out the bedroom window and there was the moon in all its eclipsed glory, blood red, with just an edging of light. I found my warm clothes and stepped out into the cold Minnesota night to take some pictures.

So beautiful.
Silent through and through – Great Peace.
Venerable Elder!
You – whoever you are.

46

How do you understand?

Yuantong, drawing a circle around them, asked:
"'Buddhas of the three times and the six Ancestors are
always right here.' How about for you?"

Wansong replied: "The overnight guest rejoices."

Linquan's Verse

The overnight guest rejoices
The day is warm, the month is cold
The four oceans accept waves
Heaven and earth are profoundly still
Master Ma confused Master Qin
As if up until today, not yet aware

Commentary

"Buddhas of the three times and the six Ancestors are always right here,"
reads like a quote, but I have not been able to locate the source. So maybe
Yuantong is just being haughty. In any case, he again challenges Wansong,
as if to say, is it really true that all the Buddhas and the six founding
Chinese Ancestors are right here? Show me.

> When this body was thirty-three, I met with my old
> teacher, Katagiri Roshi, at the Fairview-Riverside Hos-
> pital in Minneapolis. He had just been diagnosed with
> cancer and so was wrapping up some loose ends, espe-
> cially the training of his priests. Katagiri Roshi asked me
> if I would receive dharma transmission from him. "Yes,"
> I said, "but only if you live and train me for twenty more
> years." "I'll always be there with you," he said.[105]

And he has.

Wansong refers to the overnight guest, the one-night student, Yongjia,
a monk who had his enlightenment verified by the Sixth Ancestor,

---

105 Xutang Zihu, *Record of Empty Hall: One Hundred Classic Koans*, trans., Dosho Port
(Boulder: Shambhala Publications, 2021), 50.

Huineng, and spent just one night with him. If you only spent one night with your teacher, you'd be happy too that they were always there with you. Perhaps Wansong also had the story of Yongjia meeting Huineng in mind:

> On arrival, shaking his staff and carrying his water bottle, Yongjia circumambulated the Ancestor three times. The Ancestor said, "A worthy monk possesses the three thousand dignified demeanors and the eighty thousand detailed practices. Where does the great virtuous one come from, giving rise to such haughtiness of self?" Yongjia said, "The matter of birth and death is great, being impermanent and fleeting." The Ancestor asked, "Why not embody the Unborn and penetrate the non-fleeting?" Yongjia said, "Embodiment is the Unborn and penetration originally has no speed. The Ancestor said, "That's it! That's it!"[106]

When we embody the unborn and non-fleeting, all the Buddhas and Ancestors are there with us. It's so simple and direct. So peaceful just as it is: "The day is warm, the month is cold/The four oceans accept waves/ Heaven and earth are profoundly still."

The fifth and sixth lines of the verse call to mind an incident involving the eighth ancestor, Mazu, recorded in *The Sayings of Zen Master Mazu Daoyi*:

> Mazu sent a monk to deliver a letter to Master Qin of Jingshan. In the letter, he drew a single circle. Master Qin opened the letter, took a brush, and put a dot in the center. Later on, one of the monks related these events to Nanyang Huizhong. Huizhong said, "That Jingshan, he fell for Mazu's set-up."[107]

The overnight guest got it right away. Master Qin fell for the set-up. In between a whole lifetime of joys and sorrows.

---

106 Daoyuan, *Record of the Transmission of the Lamp*, vol. 2, *The Early Masters*, trans., Rudolph S. Whitfield (Printed in Germany: Books on Demand, 2015), 116. Modified.

107 Mazu Daoyi, *Master Ma's Ordinary Mind: The Sayings of Zen Master Mazu Daoyi*, trans., Fumio Yamada (Somerville, MA: Wisdom, 2017), 101.

47

What side of the matter?

With his hand, Yuantong made a dot in space and asked: "What side of the matter is this little dot on?"

Wansong replied: "Guizong is still here."

Linquan's Verse

Guizong is still here
Two winners, one game
This side, no obstruction
The other side, no hindrance
Always write the eight dharmas, observing thoroughly
During the time of former generations, it was already
   shared

Commentary

A government official asked Guizong, "What side's experience does the canon explain?" Guizong raised a fist and said, "Understand?" The official said he didn't understand. Guizong said, "This poor scholar doesn't even recognize a fist."[108]

Yuantong makes reference to this dharma encounter in his question. Ah, this ephemeral life! A fist or a dot in space – is it form or is it emptiness? This little dot is also the point of departure for a reflection on one of the most subtle points in Zen practice, embodied by the Wild Fox koan, and Linquan is on it.

Linquan's second line of verse, "Two winners, one game," 兩彩一賽, brings in a phrase used elsewhere in our Zen literature. We might think that there is just one right answer, that this dot in space is just on one side of the matter, but this either/or mind is itself the world of suffering in the swirl of cause and effect.

And that brings us to the Wild Fox koan with its present Baizhang and former Baizhang meeting face-to-face through a wild fox intermediary (just like Yuantong is manifesting the past Guizong in his pres-

---

108 Thomas Cleary, Thomas, *One Hundred Questions: A Chan Buddhist Classic*, Kindle Edition, 50.

ent body). The second line of Wumen's verse for *No Gate Barrier*, Case 2: Baizhang's Wild Fox, is also "Two winners, one game," 兩彩一賽. I'm not a historian, so I don't know if Linquan had access to Wumen's *No Gate Barrier*, although it did precede our present text by a couple decades, so it is possible. On the other hand, Wansong & Co. were in northern China and Wumen was in the south. Even so, the same line occurring in the second line of both verses is surely suspicious, as well as the third and fourth lines ("This side, no obstruction/The other side, no hindrance") mirroring Wumen's third line. Here is Wumen's verse:

> Not avoiding, not obscuring –
> Two winners, one game.
> Not obscuring, not escaping –
> A thousand mistakes, ten thousand mistakes!

In the main case of the Wild Fox koan, we are brought into the past of great teacher Baizhang and presented with another either/or situation, much like "What side of the matter does a dot made in empty space fall on?" Here the question is "Does a great practitioner fall under the law of karma or not?" The main part of the case goes like this:

> Every time master Baizhang spoke to the assembly, an old man was there listening. When they left, he would too. Then one day, he didn't leave. Baizhang asked, "Who is this, standing here before me?" The old man said, "I am not human. In the past, in the time of Kashyapa Buddha, I lived on this mountain. Someone asked if a great practitioner even falls under the law of karma or not. Answering that such a person does not fall under the law of karma, I was born five hundred times as a wild fox. Please master, give a turning word and free me from the body of a fox. Does a great practitioner even fall under the law of karma or not?" Baizhang said, "Such a one does not obscure karma ." In these words, the old man was greatly awakened. Making his bows he said, "I have shed the body of a fox.[109]

"Not fall under/not obscure" – right here lies the subtlety of freedom that's opened through the Wild Fox koan. You might have noticed that "not fall under/not obscure" is different from the more common translations of this koan that have the first question something like this: "Does

109 Wumen Huikai, *The No Gate Barrier*, Case 2: Baizhang's Wild Fox, trans., Dosho Port (unpublished).

an enlightened person fall into karma or not?" and the former Baizhang, answering, "Such a person does not escape into karma."

Simplified, does an awakened person fall into karma? No.

This provides for a clear "wrong" answer that leads to five-hundred years as a shape-shifting, occultish, fox and stands in sharp juxtaposition with the "right" answer that leads to becoming a human being. That right answer comes next: "Such a one does not obscure karma."

The key character in the first answer is 落, commonly translated as "escape," but that I've rendered "fall under." Yes, 落 means "escape" and "fall under." So, the response by the former Baizhang can also be read like this: "Such a person does not fall under the law of karma."

Simplified, does an awakened person fall under karma? They don't fall under.

There is subtle difference between "not escape karma " and "not fall under karma." The second reading adds an important layer of subtlety to the koan. The former Baizhang's answer is (almost) exactly the same as the present Baizhang's – "not fall under" (slightly less definitive) vs. "not obscure" (slightly more definitive). For koan introspection, rendering 落 "escape" obscures the subtle difference/identity of the koan and, most importantly, the subtlety of the conundrums of this very life. Rendering 落 as "fall under" exposes this radical and subtle shift in meaning and (almost) collapses the distinction between the "wrong" answer that led to a ghoulish ground-hog's-day rebirth in karma and the "right" answer that leads to freedom as a practicing human being.

In so-called real life, wrong and right are sometimes just so subtle. There are light actions, dark actions, and indeterminate actions – the great grey. You say what seems to be the right thing but get slammed – "Wrong!" Or a love that seems so right, but for the wrong person just leads to swirling in pain. "Go directly to five-hundred lives as a wild fox!"

And sometimes in life, it seems that there are just two choices – both wrong.

Then, even a person of great practice falls down by, oh-so-subtly avoiding, evading, obscuring the vital truth of this life right before us now – wrong and wrong. This points to the need for great practice, because only such great practice can turn the subtlety of suffering and clearly hear and see the cries of the world.

And that's the place, within the subtle, changing faces of right and wrong, that this koan really becomes a koan worthy of our attention, life after life. As Wumen comments, "If in regards to this you can succeed in obtaining a single eye, you will learn how the former Baizhang gained five-hundred rebirths of elegance."[110]

Yes, it is great practice as a wild fox, or as a Zen teacher, or as you

110 Ibid.

whoever you are, that makes this very life a life of elegance, where there are two winners for this one game. Like Linquan said in the verse, "This side, no obstruction/The other side, no hindrance/Always write the eight dharmas, observing thoroughly/During the time of former generations, it was already shared."

Appropriately, it isn't clear which "eight dharmas" we should be writing and observing. Linquan leaves out the important middle modifying character that might narrow the field, so we're left with numerous sets of eight dharmas in the list-oriented buddhadharma. For example, he could be referring to the eight essential dharmas: instruction, principle, awareness, wisdom, practice, awakening, cause, and fruit. Or he might be referring to the eight worldly dharmas: gain, loss, pleasure, pain, fame, disgrace, praise, and blame.

Because these are offered to us by previous generations, including former Baizhangs, present Baizhangs, former Guizhongs, present Guizhongs, and all wild foxes, all with their struggles and elegance, let us write out both the worldly and essential dharmas, and observe them constantly.

Many winners, one game.

48

What knowledge did your kind return with?

Yuantong asked: "For going through the door of not-going, a person sitting in the hall just won't do it. What knowledge did your kind return with?"

Wansong replied: "The continent is vast, the dragon's tail is short."

Linquan's Verse

The continent is vast, the dragon's tail is short
Contentious youth are like trembling pines
Not borrowing Lord She's brush
Why seize Mr. Ge's staff?
When in the hall, make no "I" footprint
The whole universe exposes the state of things
Compare transcending thinking to this place
One thousand peaks together with ten thousand peaks

Commentary

How are you going to go through the door of not-going?

Sit on your butt in the zendo? How could sitting still move one through?

Haven't you heard? *The Diamond Sutra* says,

> "Subhuti, if someone says that the Thus-come One comes, goes, sits, or lies down, this person does not understand the point of my teaching. Why? The Thus-come One has no place from whence they come, and no place to go. Therefore they are called 'Thus-come.'"[111]

And yet the awakened ones in each generation, sat in the hall until they broke through their zazen cushions, went through and kept going. Granted, most of those who have broken through, both ancients and moderns,

---

111 *The Diamond Sutra*, trans., Charles Muller, http://www.acmuller.net/bud-canon/diamond_sutra.html#div-23.

have not done so while sitting in the hall. Dogen and Keizan are notable exceptions. Sitting in the hall, though, is highly correlated with breakthroughs.

What advice does one of those thoroughly thus-gone ones, Wansong, have for us?

"The continent is vast, the dragon's tail is short."

This trembling pine is so tall. That trembling pine is so short.

Thus-gone one Linquan chimes in with some advice too, first with the lines "Not borrowing Lord She's brush/Why seize Mr. Ge's staff?" Cleary explains that

> Lord She's brush refers to an artist whose depictions of dragons were considered extremely realistic. Mr. Ge's cane refers to a Taoist legend of a wizard whose cane turned into a dragon on which he rode off to infinity.[112]

It is best to become humble, not as a practice, but from the experience of trembling. Let go of what you think you have. In the practice hall, hide yourself in the rule, but not in transcendence. The great intimacy can be revealed through anything. One thousand hairy heads together with ten thousand hairy heads.

As for "The whole universe exposes the state of things/Compare transcending thinking to this place," Linquan celebrates the power of wisdom. Shutting up completely is cool, but that's not the fruit of the bodhi tree.

---

112 Thomas Cleary, *One Hundred Questions: A Chan Buddhist Classic*, Kindle Edition, 51.

49

Why not dwell in the true position?

Yuantong asked: "Why does a person who has released their grip of the transcendent realm not abide in the true position?"

Wansong replied: "It is a great service not to rule."

Linquan's Verse

> It is a great service not to rule[113]
> As if the voice emits light
> Kick over the bed of nirvana
> Turn over and stomp on the tranquil ocean
> Freedom is everywhere when you stop grasping the
>   handle!
> Seize the true, release the biased – there is hardship in the
>   hue of the supernormal
> Then, at once, the road returns home
> A prognosticator augurs in vain[114]

Commentary

As the saying goes, Zen is like soap. First, you wash with it, then you wash it off. Yuantong asks, in effect, what's left after you wash it off?

After letting go of our grip of going beyond, isn't that absence of rank the true rank, the true position?

"Your majesty, please put on your sweatpants and sit in the back row."

Going beyond buddha is to bend oneself even more into the ordinary.

"True position," 正位, here refers to advanced practitioners who have thoroughly embodied dharma nature. Linji describe the true position as the true person of no rank, 無位真人:

> "There is a true person of no rank, always going in
> and out through the gates of your face. Those with a

---

113 Cleary says this is a quote is from the *Tao Te Ching*. See Thomas Cleary, *One Hundred Questions: A Chan Buddhist Classic*, Kindle Edition, 53.

114 Ibid. I follow Cleary here for this difficult line.

beginner's mind who have not yet proven this, look, look!"[115]

This true person is just going through the gates of the face! Then, what about "As if the voice emits light/Kick over the bed of nirvana/Turn over and stomp on the tranquil ocean/Freedom is everywhere when you stop grasping the handle!"? Well-earned praise and delight. Time to dance along the shore of the Great Lake in the soft red light of dawn with pure joy and thoroughgoing release.

And, yet, there still is subtle suffering in the place with the color of such profound practice or as Linquan says, "Seize the true, release the biased – there is hardship in the hue of the supernormal."

True freedom comes from letting go and letting go of letting go. Ah, our true home was right here on the road all along. Right here in being with whatever requires our care. For Wansong and Linquan, it was that pesky prognosticator, Yuantong, asking question after question.

---

115 Wansong Xingxiu, *The Record of Going Easy*, Case 38: Linji's True Person, trans., Dosho Port (unpublished).

50

Why not fall into this side?

Yuantong asked: "A person whose head is turned to this side, why don't they fall into this side."

Wansong replied: "No government is of great merit."[116]

Linquan's Verse

No government is of great merit
The whole country praises the extraordinary
A cool breeze blows through the dark red boundary
The bright moon seals the cinnabar entrance to the
    ancient palace
Exactly, the phenomena's inner pattern!
Originally there is no gap
Exactly, the source of the real is the conventional!
Their roots are not separate from each other
From a singular verification, the untaught wisdom
The universal function circumambulating the human
    world is unchanging

Commentary

Yuantong raises a very similar question to his last one: "Why does a person who has released their grip of the transcendent realm not abide in the true position?" Once a practitioner has entered the transcendent realm, the realm of real reality, and then "Kick[s] over the bed of nirvana/Turn[s] over and stomp[s] on the tranquil ocean," doesn't this lead to attachment to this side, the side of differentiation?

Well, no, not if we allow ourselves to be transformed in nondoing, letting go of management and control. To plumb the depths of Zen, and really be of supreme use for all the many beings, we bend ourselves, as I mentioned in the last chapter, to become even more ordinary. The post-kensho process of sitting useless zazen allows for the inner pattern to show through the phenomenal, as does the working through of subtle koan after subtle koan with a skilled teacher. In community life, it means

116 Cleary says this is a quote from *Tao Te Ching*. Thomas Cleary, *One Hundred Questions: A Chan Buddhist Classic*, Kindle Edition, 53.

receiving as much feedback from teachers, co-practitioners, family, and friends as we can stand.

> Originally there is no gap
> Exactly, the source of the real is the conventional!
> Their roots are not separate from each other.

And so there is nothing to do but roll up our sleeves and go to work.

Wansong and Linquan seem to be patiently laying out the path of practice to be pursued for Yuantong, who seems to be asking questions that are beyond his level of experience. We know from Linquan's preface that he didn't realize definitive awakening until after he'd asked his one hundred questions. It seems important to return to what Linquan shared there about Yuantong's process with Wansong:

> Through the upright application of samadhi, Yuantong experienced supernormal cognition. After waiting patiently to verify him, Wansong transmitted the dharma to him.

In contemporary terms, this is the kensho and post-kensho process of refining and actualizing the glimpse of true nature. Linquan returns to this process in the ninth line of the verse: "From a singular verification, the untaught wisdom."

Verification occurs in the teacher-student relationship in many ways, formal and informal, including the passing through of initial and break-through koan, and then all the way through the completion of the koan curriculum and dharma transmission.

Dogen works through this territory in his "Going Beyond Buddha," first by raising this utterance from Zen Master Baoji: "The single path of going beyond – a thousand sages, no transmission."

Dogen comments:

> It means that even if thousands of sages appear all to-gether, the single path of going beyond is not transmit-ted. No transmission means a thousand sages protect that which is not transmitted. You may be able to un-derstand in this way. But there is something further to say about this. It is not that a thousand sages or a thou-sand wise people do not exist, but that a single path of going beyond is not merely the realm of the sages or of the wise.[117]

---

117 Eihei Dogen, *Treasury of the True Dharma Eye: Zen Master Dogen's Shobo Genzo,*

Face-to-face verification culls out what cannot be transmitted, what must be protected. This is the untaught wisdom, 無師智. The process of verification in our Zen Way is powerful and has no boundary. The door for ongoing traceless practice opens. "The universal function circumambulating the human world is unchanging."

"Going Beyond Buddha," trans., Kazuaki Tanahashi (Boulder: Shambhala Publications, 2010), 320.

51

Why do the upright and intimate suffer the stick?

Yuantong asked: "Seven vertical and eight horizontal, through a person's thousand changes, ten thousand changes. Why do the upright and intimate suffer the stick?"

Wansong replied: "Almost slipped by."

Linquan's Verse

> Almost slipped by conferring the whole thing
> Suitable marvelous function, the fruit of generosity, is
>   certainly unusual
> Seeing the truth, but not acting, lacks courage
> Knowing what has been done for you, straightforwardly
>   announcing your devotion
> A beautiful narrow path with thorns in the mud
> The virtuous meet a coarse, argumentative, bloodless
>   person
> Like guarding a money bag with a hole in it
> Thus we know that dull iron wears out the tongs and
>   hammer of an adept

Commentary

"Seven vertical and eight horizontal," moving this way and that through the wild ranges of daily life, refers to the free functioning of a person of great practice. And yet such a person, upright and intimate, still gets beaten. And even suffers the blows of the staff from their Zen teacher. Or if their teacher is out of range, then from any of the many beings. I've taken a few shots myself, mostly invited by my own errant proclivities.

But enough about me – who is it that almost slipped by Wansong? As was discussed earlier, Yuantong is not at the place in his practice for marvelous function, so perhaps Wansong is making a side comment about his attendant, Linquan, who has been transparent in these dialogues. I see Linquan sitting quietly through the exchanges, pouring tea, adjusting the blinds on the windows, and then after Wansong has gone off to bed, he straightens the cushions, cleans up from tea, then goes off to his room to jot down notes about the question and answer. Later, perhaps much later, he then tacks on these verses, or swamp songs as he calls them.

One slip the teacher can make is sharing the whole thing and not leaving anything for the student to realize on their own. Wumen put this point like this:

> By chance, meeting a person, just speak three parts.
> Don't give the whole thing at once.[118]

The next three lines of verse acknowledge the conundrum of a person of great practice: "Suitable marvelous function, the fruit of generosity, is certainly unusual/Seeing the truth, but not acting, lacks courage/Knowing what has been done for you, straightforwardly announcing your devotion."

Given the complexities of this life and the flow of impermanence, marvelous function that fits exactly with the circumstances is rare, even for those whose dharma eye is wide open and clear. Even the great Harada Tangen Roshi stumbled from time to time.

But seeing what is true, and feeling deep gratitude for those that have gone before, it is simply necessary to try to help. Anything else reflects a lack of gratitude.

The fifth line pointedly wraps up the first movement of the verse – there are thorns in the soft, warm mud of this beautiful path. Linquan here seems to be speaking from experience.

Perhaps Wansong is also referring to himself as the guy who almost slipped by and Yuantong and Linquan are then representatives of coarse, argumentative, bloodless students. The teacher keeps an eye on them as what's precious drains away. In these last lines Linquan steps into Wansong's body and speaks: "Like guarding a money bag with a hole in it/ Thus we know that dull iron wears out the tongs and hammer of an adept."

The "tongs and hammer of an adept" refer to undertaking rigorous training under a Zen master, or in this case offering rigorous training, often likened to the alchemical smelting process, turning lead into gold. In this context, the master uses tongs to hold the person in the container of training and the hammer to pound the person into a more useful form. A coarse, argumentative, and bloodless person is transformed into a Buddha.

A limitation of this metaphor for training is how it puts a good deal of the work on the side of the teacher. Is the student passive, like dull iron

---

118 Wumen Huikai, *The No Gate Barrier*, Case 33: Not Mind, Not Buddha, trans., Dosho Port (unpublished).

on the anvil? No, the students' job is to be coarse, argumentative, and bloodless. That takes a lot of work.

The Zen master takes on the coarse person, watching them as one would watch a money bag that leaks coins, knowing that the tongs and hammer of their teaching life will be worn out through the process. What's the alternative? Save the tongs and hammer for what?

Seeing that a living being is already Buddha and not acting is cowardice.

52

What reward is there?

Yuantong asked: "A person's one hundred achievements, a thousand undertakings, what reward is there?"

Wansong replied: "Zhaozhou tea. Caoshan wine."

Linquan's Verse

Zhaozhou tea. Caoshan wine.
Not necessary to boil water, there is a method for
 constant brewing
Obstructed by two cups of tea and three cups of wine,
 the thirsty arrive
Won't hurt to sober up after seventy or eighty pints
If a bit unfulfilled, offer more of it
Afraid to accept, send the flavor to the disciple's open
 mouth

Commentary

"All dharmas are marked by emptiness," says *The Heart Sutra*, and further, that there is "no attainment." If so, there is no reward and no one to receive it. Then why toil through a thousand activities with a hundred achievements and nine hundred failures?

In response, Wansong serves up Zhaozhou tea and Caoshan wine. Zhaozhou's tea refers to this story:

> Zhaozhou questioned two new arrivals. The master asked the first one, "Have you been here before?" The monk said, "No, I haven't." The master said, "Go have some tea." The master then asked the other monk. "Have you been here before?" The monk said, "Yes, I have." The master said, "Go have some tea." The monk asked, "Setting aside the fact that you told the one who'd never been here before to go have some tea, why did you tell the one who had been here before to go have some tea?" The master said, "Head monk!" The head monk said,

"Yes?" The master said, "Go have some tea."[119]

Caoshan's wine refers to this koan:

> A monk asked Caoshan, "Qingshui is alone and poor. I beg you master please help." Shan said, "Monk Shui!" Shui answered, "Yes?" Shan said, "You've had three cups of the household wine, yet say you have not yet moistened your lips."[120]

What is Wansong's point? If you're worried about what you're going to get, you don't realize that you've already gotten it. You're already drunk, so go have some tea.

This tea is constantly brewing without artifice or contrivance. This wine is *form is exactly emptiness*. The barrier is the thirst. When are you going to have enough of what you already are?

With nothing to attain, a bodhisattva relies on prajna paramita and thus the mind is without hindrance. Without hindrance, there is no fear.

Meanwhile, you're drunk, so go have a cup of tea.

119 Zhaozhou Congshen, *The Recorded Sayings of Zen Master Joshu*, trans., James Green (Boston: Shambhala Publications, 1998), 146. Modified.

120 Wumen Huikai, *The No Gate Barrier*, Case 10: Qingshui Alone and Poor, trans., Dosho Port. (unpublished). Also see Wansong Xingxiu, *The Book of Serenity, The Record of Going Easy*, Case 38 Linji's True Person, trans., Dosho Port (unpublished). Wansong also mentions the case in his commentary to *The Book of Serenity: One Hundred Zen Dialogues*, Case 73: Caoshan's Fulfillment of Filial Piety, trans., Thomas Cleary (Boulder: Shambhala Publications, 2005), 307-310.

53

What point is most intimate?

Yuantong asked: "Fengxue's Five Correct Points – what point is most intimate?"

Wansong replied: "This point is most intimate."

Linquan's Verse

> This point is most intimate
> The true mind expresses the true
> A shining disclosure of a *kesa*-wearing monk's nostrils[121]
> Enhancing the spirit of new buddha ancestors
> Establishing the dharma banner in reality
> Laying down the fundamental meaning in a speck of dust
> The conjecture of ordinary consciousness is infinite
>   wisdom
> How many people directly and completely pass through?

Commentary

Fengxue Yanzhao (896-993) was the fourteenth-generation successor in China through Nanyuan Huiyong (860-930), and three generations after Linji. All the Linji/Rinzai lineages that survive today trace their ancestry through Fengxue. He once said,

> The function of the ancestors' mind seal is like the Iron
> Ox. Remove the seal and it remains. If it remains, the
> seal is ruined. If neither removed nor remaining, is there
> a seal or not?[122]

The working of this Iron Ox brought us Fengxue's Five Correct Points that Yuantong asks about. However, once again, it isn't clear which five points Yuantong is referencing. I asked my Zen teacher friends, especially those of a Linji/Rinzai orientation, and Guo Gu Laoshi shared what he thought Yuantong might be talking about:

---

121 "Kesa" is the monk's robe, sometimes also referred to as a "patched-robe." The "kesa-wearing monk's nostrils" refers to the true self of the monk.

122 Yuanwu Keqin, *The Blue Cliff Record*, Case 38, trans., Dosho Port (unpublished).

1) Fengxue's ability to penetrate disciples' attached views (破執). He said himself that this was his primary task whenever someone came to him for teachings.

2) Fengxue's ability to reveal the realization of awakening. There are several strategies attributed to him that are quite famous (demonstrating by shattering attachments; revealing through actions of body-mind; focusing on function; and daily life)

3) Fengxue's inheritance and wide use of Linji's Four Positions (四料簡) of Host and Guest (四賓主). He was probably the one who made Linji's method famous.

4) Fengxue was known for responding to questions through verse couplets (二句偈).

5) Fengxue usually didn't reply to questions directly, but if he did his response typically had a strong flavor of "tathagatagarbha chan" (如來藏禪) or buddhanature.[123]

Clearly, an incredible teacher with a wide-ranging arsenal at his disposal to free living beings. Which of the five is most intimate?

Before we push that point, though, I'd like to include Thomas Cleary's perspective. He thinks that Yuantong is referring to an incident that occurred when Fengxue met his teacher, Nanyuan, and he checked his teacher five times:

> When Fengxue first met his teacher, skipping the customary courtesies he immediately asked, "When entering the door one must discern the host. I directly request the teacher to distinguish." Nanyuan put his left hand on his knee. Fengxue shouted. Nanyuan then put his right hand on his knee. Fengxue shouted again. Nanyuan raised his left hand and said, "I grant you this one." Then he raised his right hand and said, "And what about this one?" Fengxue said, "Blind." Nanyuan went to pick up his staff. Fengxue said, "What are you doing? I'll take away the staff and hit you – don't say I didn't tell you." Nanyuan said, "I've been an abbot for thirty years – today I've had a yellow-faced riverlander come to my door and frame me."[124]

---

123 From electronic correspondence (Facebook message) with Guo Gu, December 8, 2020.

124 Thomas Cleary, *One Hundred Questions: A Chan Buddhist Classic*, Kindle Edition, 56.

What point is most intimate? It certainly is a set up!

The character that I've translated as "intimate," 親, suggests a sense of affection and familiarity. So, in addition to which point is most intimate, Yuantong is also asking which point is closest to Fengxue's family style of Zen.

Wansong cuts through it all, "This point is most intimate."

Rather than feeding the dispersive tendencies of the divided mind, Wansong rolls the meeting back to the immediate, ineffable present – just this point, the true mind just as it is, expresses the truth. Which point is that?

At just such a time, when we are intimate with our nostrils, the central feature of the original face, the kesa-wearing practitioner opens in luminousity.

The next three lines of Linquan's verse praise Fengxue: "Enhancing the spirit of new buddha ancestors/Establishing the dharma banner in reality/Laying down the fundamental meaning in a speck of dust.

"A speck of dust," refers to another penetrating koan involving Fengxue that appears in *The Record of Going Easy*, Case 34: Fengxue's One Particle of Dust, allowing many a Zennist to flourish in particular:

> Setting up one particle of dust, the entire nation flourishes. Not setting up one particle of dust, the entire nation perishes.[125]

Linquan's seventh line is a thumb in the eye of any lingering impulse to make the buddhadharma otherworldly and apart: "The conjecture of ordinary consciousness is infinite wisdom."

This point is most intimate. And yet, lost in dispersion, there is no chance to directly and completely pass through. How many people directly and completely pass through? From what I've seen, I'd say that although there won't be none, there will be few.

---

125 Wansong Xingxiu, *The Record of Going Easy*, Case 34: Fengxue's One Particle of Dust, trans., Dosho Port (unpublished).

54

Which phrase is most wonderful?

Yuantong asked: "Yunmen handed down three phrases. Which one is most wonderful?"

Wansong replied: "This phrase is most wonderful."

Linquan's Verse

This phrase is most wonderful
One sentence directly apprehended
Do not pursue right and wrong
Confusing the human realm
Zen flows with diligent care in subtle critical examination
There are very few that go beyond this remarkable ability

Commentary

One of the most luminous Zen masters in our history of luminosity is Yunmen Wenyan (864-949). Linquan's last line of verse, "There are very few that go beyond this remarkable ability," seems to eulogize Yunmen. He trained with many teachers, including a successor of Huangpo, Muzhou Daoming, who slammed a door and broke Yunmen's foot, catalyzing a deep awakening.

Later, Yunmen became a dharma heir of Xuefeng Yicun, and as a teacher was renowned especially for his capacity for one-word barriers, like "Barrier!" After he died, his successors identified three essential elements in his teaching, and so summarized his dharma with three phrases:

> Cuts off the myriad streams;
> Envelops and covers heaven and earth;
> Follows the waves, pursues the breakers.[126]

Of the first phrase, "cuts off the myriad streams," Yamada Koun Roshi writes,

> The thinking in your head is fatally hazardous to the true reality. In Yunmen's speech, you can observe the

---

126 Trans., Dosho Port (unpublished).

power to truly annihilate delusions. That's why some of his phrases have no logic at all.

Of the second phrase, "envelops and covers heaven and earth," Yamada Koun Roshi writes:

> So, if you are advanced to a certain degree in your koans, it's vital to make efforts to "knead the words," that is, weigh the best suitable expression for your understanding of the given koan. If a student has grasped the point of the koan and can present the fitting answer, it's called "intention and expression – both fulfilled" [i itari ku itaru] – the most desirable state. But there are very many cases of "intention fulfilled, expression half-baked."

Of the third phrase, "follows the waves, pursues the breakers," Yamada Koun Roshi writes:

> That is, a Zen master must face their students according to their respective degrees: highly advanced persons must be treated as advanced persons, beginners as beginners. The master's method must perfectly suit each practitioner.[127]

Yuantong wants to know which of the three phrases is most wonderful. When received wholly and completely with an open heart, how could it be a phrase other than this one?

How? If we're pursuing right and wrong, that's how. Oh, so confusing! Fortunately, authentic "Zen flows with diligent care in subtle critical examination." "Critical examination," 參詳 (Chinese, canxiang; Japanese, sansho), is used synonymously with the now more common 參禪 (Chinese, canchan; Japanese, sanzen), referring both to zazen and to face-to-face meeting with a Zen master, especially to critically examine a koan. In practice, it is the student's standing in this life that is critically examined.

Like I was saying, "There are very few that go beyond this remarkable ability."

---

127 Yamada Koun, *Hekiganroku (Blue Cliff Record)*, Case 14: A Preaching in Accordance, 2-3, pdf.

55

Without words, how did Buddha teach?

Yuantong asked: "Buddha didn't speak a single word. How did his teaching fill the dragon palace?"

Wansong replied: "Two words, three words."

Linquan's Verse

> Two words, three words
> This meaning is no meaning
> Prajna is the true source
> Wonderful wisdom has no teacher
> Seeing yellow leaves stops children from crying
> Scrape off your raised eyebrow – stop conjecturing

Commentary

The Buddha too said he didn't speak a single word. You might reasonably wonder who it was that yammered away through the 84,000 sutras and commentaries.

The dragon palace is where the dragon king lives beneath the Eastern Sea. It's reputed to be filled with secret texts and other cool stuff. *The Lotus Sutra* has Manjushri coming from there at the beginning of the sutra and again in Chapter 12: Devadatta. That's the famous chapter where the dragon king's daughter transmogrifies to put Shariputra in his place. But the Buddha doesn't actually show up in the dragon palace so either Yuantong is in on the liberating joke or he might have some other sutra in mind.

The central issue, though, is "How is it that they speak without using their tongues?"[128] In our Harada-Yasutani koan curriculum we encounter this issue early in the process of practicing awakening and it comes up again in *The No Gate Barrier*, and again in *The Blue Cliff Record*. In the latter text, the great master Baizhang tests three of his senior students by asking, "Even though your throat, lips and mouth are shut, how will you speak?"[129]

---

128 *Entangling Vines: A Classic Collection of Zen Koans*, trans., Thomas Yuho Kirchner (Somerville, MA: Wisdom, 2013), 126.

129 Yuanwu Keqin, *The Blue Cliff Record*, Cases 70, 71, and 72, trans., Dosho Port (unpublished).

The issue also arises in *The Record of Empty Hall*, Case 3: The World-Honored One Finally Pays Attention:

> When the World-Honored One was about to enter nirvana, Manjusri asked him to turn the dharma wheel once again. The World-Honored One said, "Goodness! I've lived in this world for forty-nine years and haven't ever spoken a word. You ask me to turn the dharma wheel again. Have I ever turned the dharma wheel?"
> On behalf of Manjusri, Xutang said, "Finally, the World-Honored One is paying attention."[130]

This morning, after our breakfast of oatmeal, and before our two-hundred-foot walk to Lake Superior, my wife and I checked into the Vine of Obstacles to see how our students are doing. I moved along to respond to an email, while Tetsugan, always attentive to detail, made an observation about a student, wondering how they're doing.

As she talks, I continue to type. Then she asks, "Did you hear what I just said?"

"You didn't speak a single word," I replied with a grin.

Whether you are paying attention or not, I bet it's clear that this is a central issue in the tradition. So, believe you me, I'll also not say a word.

The true meaning is, after all, no meaning. Linquan mutters that rather than even the Buddha's words, "Prajna is the true source," and teaches that "Wonderful wisdom has no teacher." Words are likened to yellow leaves that children mistake as gold coins and so stop crying.

If you want to know for yourself how to speak without using your tongue, and I pray that you do, just "scrape off your raised eyebrow – stop conjecturing."

Or ask my wife – the Sensei.

---

130 Xutang Zihu, *Record of Empty Hall: One Hundred Classic Koans*, trans., Dosho Port (Boulder: Shambhala Publications, 2021), 26.

56

How is it for you?

Yuantong asked, "'Cause' embraces the ocean of 'effect'. 'Effect' penetrates the root of 'cause'. How do you say something apart from cause and effect?

Wansong replied, "Saying is also not saying."

Linquan's Verse

Saying is also not saying
Searching through discussion is not required
Know a person by their words
Grass can be recognized from a sprout
Haggling is not necessary to clearly understand the four
  truths
Going beyond the ten stages, do not presume to
  maintain characteristics

Commentary

One of the most critical teachings of the Buddha is that what we do and what we don't do can lead to awakening. We are not the hapless victims of our birth and of that which happens to us. Indeed, what we do is what happens to us.

We have the capacity to train, to awaken to what we already are, and to live lives of meaning, especially when our purpose is to benefit and create the conditions for the awakening of all the many beings.

Yuantong here parses cause and effect, 因果, setting up his question by first noting the identification of cause and the ocean of effect, and how the cause and effect share the same root. This juxtaposition of vast and minute is reminiscent of a couplet in Dongshan's *Jewel Mirror Samadhi*:

Fineness enters no-gap
Vastness free from direction-place[131]

After zazen this morning, we went out to see the sunrise, to be the sunrise. Fineness enters no-gap. As we turned to the path through tall lake grasses

---

131 Dongshan Liangjie, *Jewel Mirror Samadhi*, trans., Dosho Port.

and into the strip of trees that leads to our cottage, an eagle soared low at the tops of the trees. Vastness free from direction-place. In this intimacy of cause and effect, there is relief in suffering.

Yuantong then asks old Wansong how it is for him. "Saying is also not saying."

To realize the Way that is not the Way, haggling about in discussion is not necessary, and whether our words are entangled in the cause and effect of discussion or arise from embodying the ocean of effect, penetrating the root source is as clear as how a grass sprout grows into grass.

But even if we have achieved the Ten Stages of the Bodhisattva:

1. joyful,
2. immaculate/stainless,
3. luminous,
4. radiant,
5. invincible,
6. immediacy/coming face-to-face,
7. far-reaching/transcendent,
8. immovable/steadfast,
9. eminence/auspicious intellect,
10. cloud of dharma[132]

… these also must be released in the ocean of all-knowing wisdom.

---

132 Robert E. Buswell and Donald S. Lopez, Jr., *The Princeton Dictionary of Buddhism* (Princeton and Oxford: Princeton University Press, 2014), 1086. Also see Question 17.

57

Zen also no?

Yuantong asked: "Small, beginning, ending, sudden, perfect – are the Five Teachings of Zongmi and also Zen, no?"

Wansong replied: "Knowing the teaching is also not knowing."

Linquan's Verse

Knowing the teaching is also not going beyond
    discrimination and language
Don't initiate haggling
Willows stop the bubbling of the rushing current
The Milky Way is a wave of branches
Flowers of the jade forest are not different
Difference is not different
The clear-eyed kesa-wearing monk still touches the taboo
    word

Commentary

Guifeng Zongmi (780-841) was an enormously important scholar-monk in Chinese Buddhism and an ancestor in both the Huayan and Chan Schools. One of his interests, like many Chinese scholar-monks who came before him, was making sense of the wide array of teachings that were imported from India:

> The sutras were introduced into China at random, and it soon became apparent that they did not necessarily agree and sometimes even contradicted each other. Yet for the Chinese, these were all the teachings of a single figure, the historical Buddha, Shakyamuni, and were thus assumed to share a single, underlying salvific message. Commentators saw as their overriding task the uncovering of a sequence, order, or fundamental organizing principle that would show how the manifold Buddhist teachings related to one another and make

clear their essential unity. These attempts led to rival systems of doctrinal systematization or panjiao.[133]

Zongmi divided Buddha's teaching into five categories, summarized by Yuantong as small, beginning, ending, sudden, perfect. Here is a bit more detail:

1. humans and gods teaching
2. individual vehicle teaching
3. great vehicle dharma appearance teaching
4. great vehicle refuting appearances teaching
5. one vehicle manifesting nature teaching[134]

Zongmi's fifth division is the one vehicle of the *Lotus Sutra* that manifests ultimate reality. Yuantong asks if Zen teaching is in alignment with Zongmi's system. Wansong responds that knowing this teaching is also not knowing it – a real conversation stopper. Knowing it alone "doesn't go beyond discrimination and language."

What's a student to do? "Don't initiate haggling." Don't be like Yuantong! Although if you don't initiate haggling, you won't be able to see it and stop it. "Haggle," 商量, is to negotiate the price of a commodity, but in the Zen context it means to present a koan to one's teacher.

Don't scheme! Instead, you are here in the Milky Way within the flow of vastness. Let the willow branches of the buddhadharma shush your little mouth.

In the fifth line of the verse, Linquan says, "Flowers of the jade forest are not different." The "jade forest," 瓊林, has a number of connotations, including a forest covered with snow. In this context, it probably refers to "a collection of selected sentences."[135]

Within steadfastness, playing in the universe, each word is like a flower in the jade forest, even the differences between each word are covered with snow. What, then, is the word that is forbidden touched by Zen practitioners?

Wonderful!

---

133 Donald S. Lopez Jr. and Jacqueline I. Stone, *Two Buddhas Seated Side by Side: A Guide to the Lotus Sutra* (Princeton, NJ: Princeton University Press, 2019), 15-16.

134 Peter N. Gregory, *Inquiry into the Origin of Humanity: An Annotated Translation of Tsung-mi's Yuan jen lun with a Modern Commentary* (Honolulu: University of Hawai`i Press, 1995), 31.

135 *Digital Dictionary of Buddhism*, Thomas Muller, http://www.buddhism-dict.net/cgi-bin/xpr-ddb.pl?q=%E7%93%8A%E6%9E%97.

58

How not to get the father's burden?

Yuantong asked, "Do not go toward the Way, you'll return with the burden of the father. How not to get the father's burden?"[136]

Wansong replied: "Turning your head is prohibited."

Linquan's Verse

Turning your head is prohibited – one extraordinary
    phrase
Singular within the profound mystery – how many
    people know?
Still you can go unselfishly
The path of the bird, up and down, everywhere is proper

Commentary

Don't go toward the Way if you're thinking it's something pure. When we undertake this path of practice, an ancestral transmission, we find the great gifts of freedom <u>and</u> the burden of our ancestry. The inheritance is never just one sided. Those who make such claims are in denial. And headed for a fall. Awakening and delusion come together, tangled more tightly than wisteria. In addition, what was medicine for one generation is often poison for the next.

The issue applies just as well for our biological parents, of course, but today, my old dad's 91st birthday, I'm inclined to just focus on my dharma parents.

How can we practice so as not to carry our dharma parents' burden? First, identify it! And second, don't look away! Thus, Wansong says, "Turning the head is prohibited."

In my case, early on in my relationship with my root teacher, Katagiri Roshi, I was his attendant at Hokyoji during a practice period. While I was heating water for his bath in a make-shift metal drum with a gas stove underneath, he came out of his cabin and joined me sitting in the grass. I asked him about dharma transmission, and he told me that he would only

---

136 The text uses the character for father here, 父, so with gender-fair regrets, I've left it gendered in the translation and use "parent" in the commentary.

give dharma transmission in the most authentic way.

However, years later when he was diagnosed with a serious cancer, he decided to give dharma transmission to twelve of his priests. Even at the time, this seemed premature – a late in the game Hail Mary. Were all twelve of us ready for transmission in the most authentic way? I don't think so, and that includes the thirty-three year-old former Dosho. Even though Katagiri Roshi encouraged all of us to continue our training, most of the group did not.

From those twelve premature transmissions, to date, more than sixty-two people have received teaching authorization in successive generations according to the lineage chart at the Katagiri Project.[137] How many have found the authentic way, I don't know. It may not be none, but certainly it is few.

Finding an authentic successor was the burden of our parent, Katagiri Roshi, and he passed that burden on by authorizing his students prematurely.

What to do? Other than pointing this out, I can just tend to my own dharma stream, of course. Here's how I've done that: After Katagiri Roshi's death, I continued to train, practicing with nearly twenty teachers all told in the US, Europe, and Japan, and finally received inka shomei from James Myoun Ford Roshi about twenty-five years after the Katagiri transmission. In addition, I've been careful in giving dharma transmission – by not giving transmission – and I expect to die with at most a couple successors.

As Linquan says, "Singular within the profound mystery – how many people know?" Linquan also assures us that it is possible to unselfishly leave home, again and again, and live out the way of freedom. He cites the "path of the bird," referring probably to a great teacher in Wansong's lineage, Dongshan, and his three paths (the other two being the hidden path, and the path of extending hands).

> A monk asked, "You, Master, usually teach students to go the path of birds, but I wonder, what is the path of birds?" Dongshan said, "You do not encounter a single person." The monk asked, "How does one go on it?" Dongshan said, "You absolutely must go without a thread beneath your feet."[138]

How can we follow the path of the bird as it leaves no traces through the empty sky? Don't turn away! When we encounter an authentic person, an ancestral teacher even, who is encountering who?

---

137 https://www.mnzencenter.org/uploads/2/9/5/8/29581455/lineage_v.20211001.pdf

138 Keizan Jokin, *Record of the Transmission of Illumination*, Volume 2, trans., William M. Bodiford (Tokyo: Soto shu Shumucho, 2017), 209. Modified.

Zen master Hongzhi, also in the Dongshan succession, said this about the path of the bird: "It must be a place that has no footprints, where one's body is not obstructed by the slightest thread."[139]

Linquan must have been aware of Hongzhi's comment and so refers to it with "up and down, everywhere is proper." Indeed, to face and address the sins of our parents, we are always treading a path with no forebears. As long as we don't turn our heads, everywhere is proper. And yet, we can't but turn our heads, because our heads are already turned, at least a bit.

And so, I bow down in gratitude to Katagiri Roshi and Ford Roshi for having offered the milk of the buddhadharma.

---

139 Ibid., 210.

59

Where is the seat of enlightenment?

Yuantong asked: "According with the conditions, sensations pass. No conditions are not embraced, so they do not permanently dwell here on the seat of enlightenment. Yet say, where is the seat of enlightenment?"

Wansong replied: "Not identifying with the Way."

Linquan's Verse

> Not identifying with the Way – the fortunate are not
>   careless
> Tiles, stones, dense afflictions
> Nothing but our most valuable treasures
> Marvelous essence accords with exhausting a mysterious
>   line of verse
> Lands countless as dust are the same as the universal
>   functioning of old Gautama

Commentary

Being one with each and everything, receiving and embracing the flowing sensations like the Great Lake embraces snow. Like the snow makes the lakes. Everything arising and vanishing together. If so, where is the seat of enlightenment?

If you are looking for it, your attention is directed outside. The witness is there judging the seat of enlightenment versus not-the-seat of enlightenment. Thus, Wansong points to the seat of enlightenment: "Not identifying with the Way'"

Snow, sand, driftwood, shoreline, water, dense afflictions, Facebook, Fox News – when exhausted, the seat of enlightenment. The marvelous functioning of a line of verse is it. A line of prose is it. When picked up, it must be taken through to the end.

Only then is it authentically realized that "lands countless as dust are the same as the universal functioning of old Gautama."

If you stop short of this, such words are wild fox slobber dripping down your chin.

60

Where is enlightenment's exquisite flowering?

Yuantong asked: "The wondrous flower of enlightenment adorns the universe, whithersoever always dwelling in peace. Where is enlightenment's exquisite flowering?"

Wansong replied: "When you've sold everything, there is no need for money."

Linquan's Verse

> When you've sold everything, there is no need for money
> An intimate friend does not need still more repetitious
>   declarations
> Subhuti's insight indulges the ordinary
> Hungry-eyed Zen is to be pitied even more

Commentary

If enlightenment is flowering everywhere, where is it just now? Abandon the economy of exchange, of relative value. Thoroughgoing poverty offers unlimited wealth.

Linquan, as in "Question 26: Who is able to hear it?" and "Question 43: Is this guest or host?", again raises the example of intimate friends. As you may recall, this refers to an intimacy so close, for example, that the lute player's playing depends on the intimate friend's listening to the music.

Linquan holds up the example of the intimate friends as if to say that Yuantong isn't quite there yet in his relationship with Wansong. "More intimate, more intimate," he beseeches. In Question 26, Linquan said, "Intimate friends need not hold each other up again and again." In Question 43, Linquan said, "Intimate friends need not repeatedly reexamine a case." And here, Linquan says, "An intimate friend does not need still more repetitious declarations."

Throughout, the note plays just once and not again. And yet, Yuantong asks quite the same question here that he raised in "Question 59: Where is the seat of enlightenment?" Linquan points out that if Yuantong and Wansong were truly intimates, then once would be enough.

Linquan then turns to the example of Subhuti, an intimate disciple of the Buddha, renowned for understanding emptiness, and the recursive petitioner of the Buddha in *The Diamond Sutra*. As the sutra begins, we find Subhuti settled into a rut of realizing only emptiness, indulging the ordinary, but not giving his awakening away through compassionate activity.

What I've translated here as "ordinary," 常, could also be rendered "constant," or "unceasing," as in

> Zhaozhou asked Nanquan, "What is the Way?"
>
> Quan said, "Ordinary mind is the Way."
>
> Zhou asked, "Is it possible to direct oneself towards it then?"
>
> Quan said, "To intentionally try to do that directly is scheming."
>
> Zhou asked, "If not intentionally trying, how can you know the Way?"
>
> Quan said, "The Way does not belong to knowing or not knowing. Knowing is delusion, not knowing is blankness."[140]

The "ordinary" in "Ordinary mind is the Way," is this same ordinary, 常.

Qingyuan, a successor of the Sixth Ancestor whose lineage became Caodong line, once said,

> When I first began to practice, the mountains and rivers were simply mountains and rivers. After I advanced in my practice, the mountains and rivers were no longer mountains and rivers. But when I reached the end of my practice, the mountains and rivers were simply mountains and rivers again.[141]

The character, "Subhuti," is used in Zen discourse as an example of a practitioner who realized that mountains are not mountains, and rivers are not rivers, but had not yet realized that mountains are mountains, and rivers are rivers. In other words, he'd done the vital work of deconstructing the illusory world of form, indulging the ordinary, but has not yet done the equally vital reconstructive work actualizing the emptiness of emptiness.

---

140 Wumen Huikai, *The No Gate Barrier*, Case 19: The Ordinary is the Way, trans., Dosho Port (unpublished).

141 Red Pine, *The Diamond Sutra: The Perfection of Wisdom* (New York: Counterpoint, 2001), 107-108.

Subhuti as an archetype becomes complacent, rests on their laurels, that is, until they meet the Buddha archetype of *The Diamond Sutra*, here manifested as Wansong, and become a fearless bodhisattvas, and there follows a very happy ending.

The other extreme from becoming complacent is "hungry-eyed Zen," the scheming of contriving an outcome that Nanquan warns Zhaozhou, his intimate friend, against. Indeed, such Zen of the marketplace is even more pitiable.

61

Are there no Bodhisattvas of Compassion who enter the gate of the inner pattern?

Yuantong asked: "Hearing it's time to ascend to the Treasure Hall, strike the drum, clammer up the empty sky. Are there no Bodhisattvas of Compassion who enter the gate of the inner pattern?"

Wansong replied: "Lower your voice. Lower your voice."

Linquan's Verse

> Lower your voice, rise and present without false pride
> Without enmity what meritorious deeds can be born?
> Compassion, wisdom, and the resolute mind – the
>   moon's Sea of Serenity
> Deeply hear and ponder the branches of the tradition
> Fellow practitioners, stop! Do not squander time
> How can the fruit ripen if you follow sound, pursue
>   color?

Commentary

It is time to go up to the dharma hall, also known as the Treasure Hall, and demonstrate the profound meaning to the community. I wonder if there will be any Bodhisattvas of Compassion who will then penetrate the principle, the essence of the essence?

Hush it! The family treasure does not come to those who yammer away on the street corner. What is needed to taste the Sea of Serenity is compassion, wisdom, and resolution.

The phrase in the third line of Linquan's verse, "the moon's Sea of Serenity," 澄海月, is quite an eye-popper. I don't know that the Chinese in the thirteenth century had the moon surveyed. The Sea of Serenity didn't get a name in the West until 1651. But there it is in the text.

The fourth line of verse, "Deeply hear and ponder the branches of the tradition," is quite challenging to translate and so this is an especially provisional translation. "Hear and ponder," though, are two of the three strategies to realize wisdom. Meditation is the third. "Hear" refers to hearing the Buddha's teaching. "Ponder," 思, is often translated as "thinking," but has the sense of deeply reflecting on the dharma, not a nuance that "thinking" often carries.[142] "Tradition" is also "wind" and refers to the teaching style of a lineage, palpable in everyday hearing and seeing.

The same four characters that conclude the last line of the verse, "How can the fruit ripen if you follow sound, pursue color?" 隨聲逐色, are also found in a famous verse in *The Diamond Sutra* that Yuantong asks about next in Question 62, as well as "Question 92: Why follow sounds and chase colors?[143] And so I'll save a more thorough focus for a bit. For now, though, here is that verse:

> Seeking me by using form
> or seeking me by using the sound of my voice
> A person walks a mistaken path
> And cannot perceive the Tathagata[144]

Wumen in *The No Gate Barrier* also entwines his teaching with this *Diamond Sutra* verse: "In general, in practicing Zen and studying the Way one should by all means avoid <u>following sounds or pursuing colors</u>." Wumen goes on with these practice pointers for anyone who wants to realize the wisdom that blows through the trees,

> Even if by hearing sounds one becomes aware of the Way, or seeing colors one understands the heart-mind, this is ordinary and not realization. A patched-robe monk rides sounds and hides in color, every tip bright, every touch a wonder. Yet even though it is thus, say: does sound come to the ear, or does the ear go to the sound? Or forgetting both sound and silence, what would you say?[145]

These are but two examples of the many times in the branches of the Zen tradition that this phrase can be found. Seeking thusness through something outside or something inside is a waste of time. It's like heading south and expecting to see the North Star. Instead, ride sounds, hide in color.

"Fellow practitioners, stop! Do not squander time."

---

142 思, for example, is also the character in Yaoshan's koan that Dogen uses to express the heart of zazen: "Ponder not pondering. Not pondering is the how's pondering. Nonpondering – this is zazen's vital method!"

143 For one excellent translation, see http://www.acmuller.net/bud-canon/diamond_sutra.html#div-27

144 *The Diamond Sutra*, Chapter 26, trans., Dosho Port (unpublished).

145 Wumen Huikai, *The No Gate Barrier*, Case 16: The Sound of the Bell and the Seven Piece Robe, trans., Dosho Port (unpublished).

62

What is thoroughly penetrating?

Yuantong asked: "Liberation comes from cutting off emotion, penetrating sound and color. A person's luminous mind sees nature, yet this is not yet thoroughly penetrating."

Wansong replied: "Hooked by not doubting the field of activity."

Linquan's Verse

Hooked by not doubting the field of activity
Become one with delusion and enlightenment, right and
wrong
At one time, Xuansha rejected Lingyun
Who then returned for the show
You exaggerate *perfectly clear* and *extremely luminous*
My way is just like taking a nap
Rest deeply
After the rain, clouds clear from the sky, the green of the
mountain increases

Commentary

Ah! The travails of a deeply practiced, but not fully realized student.

Everybody knows that swirling in emotion is not awakening. Cut off emotion-thought! Steadfast absorption, penetrating sounds and colors, can trigger the illumination of our true nature. And yet, right there, something is missing.

"See nature," (見性; Chinese, jianxing; Japanese, kensho) is used here as an initial or partial glimpse into the mystery of what we are. Yuantong, as we know from Linquan's preface, didn't realize it definitively until sometime after he'd asked his one hundred questions. It seems, though, from the nature of many of his questions that he had experienced kensho but hadn't yet thoroughly penetrated.

Wansong's instruction is clear and subtle – doubt the very ground, not only of your absorption, but also of your kensho. Linquan completes the instruction, going beyond merely cutting off emotions and getting a glimpse of true nature, with "Become one with delusion and enlightenment, right and wrong."

Today we employ many koans to give a student the opportunity to become one with right and wrong, but how many penetrate through and through? It seems to be more common to linger in subtle intellectualizing.

Importantly, and especially for students of just-sitting Soto Zen, we see here in one short Q & A, the contemporary presumptions that the forerunner to Japanese Soto, the Chinese Caodong of which Wansong was a preeminent representative, was not about kensho or doubt. Here we find both employed with a casualness that speaks of deep familiarity.

In the third and fourth lines, Linquan's verse shifts to Xuansha Shibei (835-908), the foremost successor of great master Xuefeng, and Lingyun (n.d.). Xuansha was the third son of a poor family who fished for a living. One day when Xuansha was out fishing with his father, a storm came up and his father fell overboard. Just then, Xuansha was seized with the aspiration to realize the Buddha Way, and so immediately turned the boat around and went to a Zen monastery. For many Zen students over the centuries, this story has been the source of skeptical doubt about the Zen Way, more so even than Shakyamuni leaving his wife and young son. At least in the latter case, both Yasodhara and Rahula became arhats. Here the result was just a drowned father.

To make matters even more tangled, the incident does not appear in Xuansha's earliest biography, written just a couple decades after his death, but first seems to appear in the records of Dahui about three centuries later.[146] It was then apparently picked up in Japan and became an often-told story. I heard it from Katagiri Roshi in the late 1970's as if it were a historic fact.

Why has such a patricidal story, and a fiction at that, become such a popular saw in Zen circles?

Zen is deadly, that's why.

But I digress. Cleary connects the reference in Linquan's verse to Lingyun with the following note:

> Xuansha/Lingyun—After meditating for thirty years, Lingyun suddenly awakened one day on seeing peach blossoms. When Xuansha heard a recitation of Lingyun's verse expressing his understanding, Xuansha remarked that it was indeed on point, but he'd bet Lingyun wasn't through yet. When this was reported to Lingyun, he responded by asking whether Xuansha himself was

---

146 See Rev. Shohaku Okumura, "The 7th Chapter of *Shobogenzo*, Ikka-myoju (One Bright Jewel) Lecture (3)," Dharma Eye, no. 39, https://global.sotozen-net.or.jp/eng/dharma/pdf/37e.pdf

through yet. This story appears in case 16 of *The Empty Valley Collection*.[147]

The rest of Linquan's verse blows up Yuantong's poor-me identity-center — the "I've had a kensho, but that's not the whole thing" pity trip.

Wansong might indulge Yuantong, spending evening after evening with his questions, but you'll have to search out Linquan's secret nap place to get any help from him.

---

147 Thomas Cleary, *One Hundred Questions: A Chan Buddhist Classic*, Kindle Edition, 66.

63

How can I grasp this inner pattern of the Way?

Yuantong asked, "'Born as if putting on a jacket. Dying as if taking off pants.' How can I grasp the inner pattern of the Way like this?

Wansong replied, "Bare hands, empty fists."

Linquan's Verse

> Bare hands, empty fists is everything, no?
> Further, you must let go and return to the road
> If you can accept reality thus
> Just trust that a dharma teacher's virtues aren't solitary
> Virtues aren't solitary
> Don't be confused
> Every honored person has ten thousand provisions
> Yet as the time draws near, fear having no soul

Commentary

There are those who realize the inner pattern of the Way as naturally as pulling on a T-shirt and taking off their pants. But you, friend, may well not be like this.

So let go of every single reliance. No gloves. Nothing hidden up the sleeves. Even let go of the way you maintain the identity center, ducking and weaving to avoid the simple clear truth. If you find a teacher who has one virtue you can see, trust that there might be more. Virtues arise in relationship, that is, they are not solitary. Trust that a lack of virtue in all living beings, might just be your own lack of clear seeing.

How can we grasp the truth, the inner pattern of phenomena, in the midst of the constant flow of lifedeath? Everyone is perfect and complete, lacking nothing, and yet as the life force fades away, most of us will fear that we lack an essence.

64

Is direct seeing-through impossible?

Yuantong asked: "The past is gone. The future is yet to arrive. 'Now' is empty and quiescent. On the other hand, why, when agreeable objects of perception appear before one, is direct seeing-through impossible?"

Wansong replied: "However, know the pain and itch."

Linquan's Verse

> However, know the pain and itch
> Without hindrance, hold the prize in hand
> Begin awakening from last night's dream
> Right and wrong are in the past
> The Buddhas' and Ancestors' authority rest with Wansong
> Do not follow empty words and phrases – roll up your
>   sleeves and go to work

Commentary

An old grandma once said, "Within the [*Diamond*] *Sutra* it says, 'past mind cannot be grasped, present mind cannot be grasped, future mind cannot be grasped.' Great virtue, what is the essential point of the one mind?"[148]

This empty, quiescent moment is perfect and complete, lacking nothing. How can you get a hold of it? And why is it so difficult when things *are* going our way?

About one-hundred years before Wansong & Co., Dahui wrote many letters to householders. In four of the sixty-two saved for posterity, he also raised this issue. It holds an enormously valuable practice tool, so let's dig into it in detail.

First, here's one example of Dahui laying out the case for when things go *against* us:

> Circumstances that go against you are easy to deal with;
> circumstances that go in your direction are difficult to
> deal with. For circumstances that go against the "I," all

---

148 Wumen Huikai, *The No Gate Barrier*, Case 28: The Resounding Echo of Longtan, trans., Dosho Port (unpublished).

that is needed is the single word "patience" – quiet your mind for a while, and the circumstance will have passed.

And Dahui continues with the more difficult practice, when things are going *our way*:

> As for sense objects that go in your way – truly there's no way to evade them. You and those sense fields are like the meeting of a magnet and a piece of iron – the two of them, before you know it, fuse into one. If even inanimate things fuse like that, how much more so is it the case between the self and ignorance: the self is wholly inside the activated ignorance and is going about making its livelihood. Confronting circumstances that go in your way, as if you have no wisdom, without being aware and without knowing, you will get drawn by them into the net.[149]

When things are going our way, that is, when conditions are consistent with our self-image, our identity center, it is very difficult to see the "I." "Going our way," by the way, does not necessarily mean they are pleasant conditions, because in some way most of us identify as a self with issues. For example, if we identify as a confused person, conditions that support confusion will be ego syntonic and support the identity center. If our identity center is constructed around the core belief that we are shit, then when shit circumstances arise, the identity center is reinforced. Thus, working with ego syntonic barriers is much more subtle work than working with ego dystonic barriers.

What can we do?

The primary method is to flip that which is ego syntonic to ego dystonic. In other words, when things are going our way, get suspicious! In the moment of suspicion, things are suddenly not going our way and we can see the self-separation. So, to flip Dahui's comment, confronting circumstances that go in our way as if we have wisdom, being aware and knowing, we will not get drawn by them into the net.

Just like Wansong says, "Just know the pain or itch!"

Just raise the imperative here and now, awakening from the dream, sloughing off right and wrong, without a purification practice for ten long kalpas, just get to work and do the dishes. Or if doing the dishes is ego syntonic, then call the plumber.

---

149 Dahui Pujue, *The Letters of Chan Master Dahui Pujue,* trans., Jeffrey L. Broughton and Elise Yoko Watanabe (New York, Oxford University Press, 2017), 276. The last two sentences are my translation.

65

What is the one dharma of liberation?

Yuantong asked: "Wide learning neutralizes meaninglessness. Wide learning fully comprehends the dharma, yet say, what is the one dharma of liberation?"

Wansong replied: "In words, the meaning is lengthy."

Linquan's Verse

In words, the meaning is lengthy
By all means, avoid haggling
Not to be compared with a fly boring into waste paper
Like a termite drilling into spoiled wood
Clever person, do not be absurd
One thousand hands of great compassion are difficult to feel
The virtue of the novice who remains silent spreads like the wind

Commentary

Expecting the one dharma of liberation through wide learning is like the path of a fly digging into shitty toilet paper, like a termite drilling into wood that is already spoiled. Neither makes a positive contribution.

Talking on and on is like offering ten bucks when the price tag says fifty cents.

It's difficult to even get a feel for the one thousand hands and eyes, let alone see with one hundred thousand eyes, or hear with ten trillion ears.

The season's first significant snowfall is coming in later. The winds have been picking up through the day, but now, suddenly, have quieted down.

66

What is obtained from a human rebirth?

Yuantong asked: "'I have a single phrase that clearly exhausts the ten profound gates and six interpretations.' Still, what is obtained from a human rebirth?"

Wansong replied: "Receive."

Linquan's Verse

Receive
Cut off the myriad streams
Three profundities and three essentials
No comparison, no companions
Chrysanthemums open when the ninth day of the ninth
    month arrives
When one leaf falls, the whole world is autumn

Commentary

Yuantong leads us into a dharma dive, with dueling (and dualing) distinctions, so I begin with Wansong's advice: "Receive."

You might exhale completing from the base of the belly, and as the life-giving breath moves through the body, gently push the last bit of air from the lungs, just as if you are helping an elderly person up a hill by placing your hands on their back and gently offering support. Then receive a full inhalation.

Now begin reading slowly with this breath sponsoring awareness.

Yuantong's first sentence, 'I have a single phrase that clearly exhausts the ten profound gates and six interpretations,' sounds like a quote more than something Yuantong would pronounce before his awakening, but if so, I have not been able to locate it.

The ten profound gates, 十玄門, from Zhiyan (602-668), the second of five ancestors of the Huayan school, unpack the relationships between dependent arising and interpenetration. They are as follows:

> All things produce one another at the same time.
> The greater and lesser influence each other.
> One and many influence each other, without losing their

own peculiarities.

All things are interdependent, so that one is all and all is
one.

Explicitness and implicitness coexist.

All things influence one another, keeping good order.

All things influence one another as the jewels of Indra's
net reflect on one another endlessly.

Anything can be made an example for the explanation of
the truth of interdependence of all things.

The past, present, and future influence one another
without confusion.

Anything can be regarded as the center of the others.[150]

The six interpretations, 六相義, unpack the relationships between the
whole and the parts. They are from Fazang (643-700), the third ancestor
of the Huayan school, who said. "Each part is identical, and they are
identical because they are different." David Elstein summarizes the six as
follows:

1. Wholeness – the identity of part and whole
2. Particularity – the distinction between the parts and
    whole
3. Identity – the mutual identity between each part,
    by virtue of the fact that they together form a whole
4. Difference – the distinct functions of each part that
    allow them to form a whole
5. Integration – how the distinct parts unite as condi-
    tions for the whole
6. Disintegration – the fact that each part maintains
    its particularity while constituting the whole[151]

Yuantong uses this carefully-thought-through philosophical background
for an earthy question, "Still, what is obtained by a human rebirth?," or
"So what?" Sounds like a teenager or a very crabby Zen student on the
second night of sesshin. "What the hell am I doing here?"

With his one-character reply, 收, "Receive," Wansong cuts through it
all. 收 also suggests "withdraw," which also might be meant here. Muller
interprets 收 in a dharma context as "To encompass one's discriminating
mind and works of letters with perfect freedom," which also applies to

---

150 *Digital Dictionary of Buddhism*, Charles Muller, http://www.buddhism-dict.net/
cgi-bin/xpr-ddb.pl?q=%E5%8D%81%E7%8E%84%E9%96%80

151 https://en.wikipedia.org/wiki/Fazang

what we're rolling in here with Yuantong.[152]

Linquan first re-embodies his teacher's one word, "Receive," and then cites one of Yunmen's three phrases, like in "Question 54: Which phrase is most wonderful?", to back him up, "Cut off the myriad streams!"

Linquan then offers Yuantong more of the same as medicine for his disease, like "Maybe if I gag the guy with it, then he'll get it!" But he also limpidly manifests the life-giving entanglements of a human rebirth.

First, Linquan cites Linji's three profound methods for training disciples:

The three profundities are: (1) 'profundity-in-essence,' realizing the ultimate truth through words which describe it; (2) 'profundity-in-phrase,' realizing the ultimate truth through words which are beyond conception; (3) 'profundity-in-profundity,' words of the ultimate truth which are beyond all forms of concept, whether affirmative or negative.

Then Linquan cites Linji's sixth generation successor, Fenyang Shanzhao's (947-1024) three essentials:

1. 'the first essential,' is words of non-discrimination;
2. 'the second essential,' is the essential into which all the enlightened sages pass; and
3. 'the third essential,' is the essential beyond verbal expressions.[153]

Linquan's fourth line of verse, "No comparison, no companions," seems to refer and prefer Linji's three profundities and Fenyang's three essentials to Zhiyan's ten profound gates and Fazang's six interpretations. In any case, after having cited Zhiyan, Fazang, Yunmen, Linji, and Fenyang, Linquan has broken into a sweat, he's rubbing his hands together, and staggering to a conclusion. Digging deep into his dharma-reference bag, he comes up with ... a holiday, the Double Ninth Festival, celebrated for a couple thousand years, where people visit the graves of their ancestors, climb mountains, and indulge in purifying beverages like chrysanthemum liquor.

"Chrysanthemums open when the ninth day of the ninth month arrives/When one leaf falls, the whole world is autumn."

What is obtained from a human rebirth?

If it's not yet obvious, just take another breath.

---

152 *Digital Dictionary of Buddhism*, Charles Muller, http://www.buddhism-dict.net/cgi-bin/xpr-ddb.pl?q=%E6%94%B6

153 *The Digital Dictionary of Buddhism*, Thomas Muller, http://www.buddhism-dict.net/cgi-bin/xpr-ddb.pl?q=%E4%B8%89%E7%8E%84%E4%B8%89%E8%A6%81

67

Where is the treasure land?

Yuantong asked: "Within the non-abiding phantom city, arrive directly in the treasure land. Yet say, where is the treasure land?"

Wansong replied: "In this place there are not two ounces of gold."

Linquan's Verse

> In this place there are not two ounces of gold
> Much like raising your voice to stop an echo
> The pearl in your clothes is clearly obvious
> Just the tinkling of jewelry as you stagger along,
> cleansed by being blown about in the whirlwind
> If you still do not know this place
> I'll immediately block your path,
> and with an open hand, smack your cheek

Commentary

Especially in this chapter, any words I might add are like frost on top of snow, raising my voice to stop an echo. Or two ounces of gold where everything is precious.

Still, there are two references to *The Sutra of the Lotus Flower of the Wonderful Dharma*, or *The Lotus Sutra* for short, and helping you connect you with these might support your reflection on this chapter. So, I'll provide some background and then quietly sneak out of the chapter.

But just one comment first. *The Lotus Sutra* does not seem to have been very important in Indian Buddhism, nor does it have the same place in the Tibetan tradition that it holds in East Asia. I once asked Katagiri Roshi what his favorite sutra was and he said without blinking an eye, "*Lotus*; what is your favorite sutra?" he teased.

"*Avatamsaka Sutra*," I replied.

"Yes," he said, "anyway, pretty intellectual."

Since that encounter, I've asked six or seven Japanese Soto priests what their favorite sutra is, and they've all said, also without hesitation, "*Lotus*." So, it seems that the *Lotus* has not only been important in East

Asia, but that it still resonates deeply with many practitioners there.

But back to our *Lotus* parables. The non-abiding phantom city and the treasure land refer to "Chapter 7: The Parable of the Magic City." Near the end of this long chapter, the Buddha tells about a large group of people who wanted to go to a place of rare treasures. It was a long journey through a wild, difficult, deserted place. And sure enough, along the way, the group becomes exhausted and disenchanted. Their wise guide conjures up a phantom city where the group can rest. When they are well-rested, the guide makes the phantom city disappear and discloses that the real treasure is near at hand. The sutra explains,

> The Buddha is just like that guide who, in order to provide a place for the travelers to rest, conjured up a great [phantom city] and, after they had rested, told them: "The place of treasures is close. This city is not real, but only something I conjured up."[154]

It is quite striking that although the phantom city and the treasure land are distinct in the sutra, Yuantong shows his Zen depth by asking how to find the treasure *within* the phantom city: "Within the non-abiding phantom city, arrive directly in the treasure land. Yet say, where is the treasure land?"

The second reference to *The Lotus Sutra* is in Linquan's verse, where he cites another well-known parable, this one from "Chapter 8: The Five Hundred Disciples Receive the Prediction of Their Destiny." In this parable, someone goes to a dear friend's house and parties through the night, eventually falling asleep. Their friend is wealthy and sews a precious jewel into their clothing, thinking that they will then have it when they need it. Waking up, this someone wanders the world, destitute and in utter poverty, until one day, they again meet their friend. The moral of the story is summed up in this portion of the verse:

> Later the friend who gave [them] the jewel
> Happened to meet this poor [person].
> Sternly rebuking [them],
> [They] showed [them] the jewel sewed into the robe.
> Seeing this jewel,
> The poor [person] was filled with a great joy.
> Being rich in valuables and other goods,
> [They] could satisfy the five desires.
> This is how we were too.

---

154 *The Lotus Sutra: A Contemporary Translation of a Buddhist Classic*, trans., Gene Reeves (Somerville, MA: Wisdom Publications, 2008), 199.

For long, the World-Honored One
Constantly took pity on us and taught us
To cultivate the highest aspiration.
But because of our ignorance
We neither perceived nor knew this.
Having gained just a little bit of nirvana,
We were satisfied and sought no more.[155]

Linquan reframes our wandering in poverty: "The pearl in your clothes is clearly obvious/Just the tinkling of jewelry as you stagger along/cleansed by being blown about in the whirlwind."

155 Ibid., 217.

68

What is true?

Yuantong asked: "'All things possess characteristics. All of them are empty and false.' Then what is true?"

Wansong replied: "Do not fancy illusory thoughts."

Linquan's Verse

Do not fancy illusory thoughts
Even more, do not produce fabrications
Vital wisdom completely interpenetrates true and false
Grasp afflictions as awakening
Greed, anger, and ignorance – nothing but the path
Regarding arrival in the crooked, distinguish
    investigation and suppression

Commentary

"'All things possess characteristics. All of them are empty and false.'" These two sentences, 凡所有相皆是虛妄, are from *The Diamond Sutra*, "Chapter 5: Physical Characteristics of Buddhahood." The whole chapter reads as follows:

> "Subhuti, what do you say? Can one discern the Tathagata by means of his bodily characteristics?" "No, World-Honored One. One cannot see the Tathagata by means of bodily characteristics. Why not? The bodily characteristics taught by the Tathagata are actually not bodily characteristics." The Buddha said to Subhuti: "All things that have characteristics are false and ephemeral. If you see all characteristics to be non-characteristics, then you see the Tathagata."[156]

The Tathagata is the one who comes thus. It is what is true. And when we see what is coming and going as not having characteristics, and not coming and going, we see truly. To see and do otherwise is simply to fancy illusory thoughts and produce fabrications.

---

156 *The Diamond Sutra*, trans., Charles Muller, 2013. http://www.acmuller.net/bud-canon/diamond_sutra.html

The buddha nature is not found apart from this very greed, anger, and ignorance. This seeing of the true in characteristics that are non-characteristics, afflictions as awakening, is a dharma path of radical intimacy, a vital wisdom that is completely hopping along, interpenetrating truth and fiction.

When embodying the crooked, the twisted, and the wrong in this way, don't use it as a form of violence to suppress the utter rawness of it all.

Investigate!

69

What about the thirty-two marks?

Yuantong asked: "All beings have a physical existence, and each and every one is impure. Yet, what do you say about the thirty-two marks?"

Wansong replied: "Break through the painting of a water bottle."

Linquan's Verse

> Break through the painting of the water bottle
> As if intoxicated, immediately sober up
> The sixteen-foot golden body
> Manifesting forms according to the capacities of living
>   beings
> Limpid autumn waters, pure suchness, the blue-green eye
>   of a monk
> The deep color of dawn in the mountains is like the dark
>   blue of the Buddha's head

Commentary

Yuantong seems to have been running to his room after his encounters with Wansong and digging into *The Diamond Sutra*. For this evening's dharma encounter he references "Chapter 13: Naming of the Sutra":

> "Subhuti, what do you think? Can the Tathagata be discerned by means of his thirty-two bodily characteristics?" "No, he cannot, World-Honored One. One cannot discern a Tathagata by means of his thirty-two bodily characteristics. And why not? Because the thirty-two bodily characteristics that are taught by the Tathagata are in fact not characteristics. Therefore, they are called the thirty-two characteristics."

What is basic to the teaching of the individual save-your-own-ass vehicle – the body as impure with all it's spit, pus, piss, and shit – meets the thirty-two marks of the compassionate carrying-all-beings-across Buddha.

What do you say about that?

"That's your thinking, always," Katagiri Roshi said to me repeatedly, so I'll repeat it here (also see "Question 18: What conditions 'no place not known'?"). But if you see your thinking and do a cognitive reframe, for example, instead of thinking that the incoming storm with all the snow we'll have to shovel and how difficult it'll be just to drive a few miles to town sucks, to, oh, it's really bright and beautiful, you're just quitting bourbon but taking up whiskey.

In either case, you, dear practitioner, are sloshy drunk. Sober up! Wake up!

"Break through the painting of the water bottle." What's real? The whole world is constantly explaining what's true according to our capacity to receive.

> Limpid autumn waters
> pure suchness
> the blue-green eye of a monk

The last line of verse – "The deep color of dawn in the mountains is like the dark blue of the Buddha's head" – compares the deep color of dawn in the mountains with the dark blue of the Buddha's head, one of the thirty-two marks.[157]

What do you mean, impure?

---

157 As amended to the traditional list by Furthest Everlasting Stream tradition. https://studybuddhism.com/en/advanced-studies/lam-rim/refuge/the-32-major-marks-of-a-buddha-s-physical-body

70

There is superior and inferior, no?

Yuantong asked: "Zen is divided into five branches. Yet there is superior and inferior, no?"

Wansong replied: "Inferior is then without-distinctions inferior."

Linquan's Verse

Inferior is then without-distinctions inferior
We must not part from each other
Jug, plate, hairpin, bracelet
'Body" is synonymous with "branch"
"Good morning!" perfectly penetrates many mouths
Many face upward, admiring the highest peak, and
    engage in superfluous talk
It's for the sovereign to decide
In the sixth month, when the sun rises, the temperature
    rises.

Commentary

"We must not part from each other" – what a wonderful perspective on our religious differences.

The five major branches in the Zen school of mid-13th century China were the Linji, Guiyang, Caodong, Yunmen, and Fayan lines, although the historians say that at least two of the five were already extinct – the Guiyang and Fayan lines. In our day, just the Linji and Caodong survive, better known, perhaps, by their Japanese names, Rinzai and Soto.

Just like a household is made from many parts – jug, plate, hairpin, bracelet – so the Zen school is made from branches that are synonymous with the body of the school. Like various everyday things – jug, plate, hairpin, bracelet – are made from one substance. So Baling, a successor in the Yunmen line, said, "Each branch of coral upholds the moon."

And yet, it's just natural for there to be high and low, superior and inferior, right? So, which is which? Which branch is the clearest, most direct pointer?

Linquan is unwilling to take a stand, "It's for the sovereign to decide." Saying, in effect, that's above my pay grade. Notably, in the introduction to the present work, he wasn't so restrained:

> Linji's key for the warp and weft gets the mystery, yet his
> tongue had no heart. Yunmen's words turned everything
> into gold, yet he didn't grasp Dongshan's biased and
> true. Neither established pure and serene gain and loss.

Wansong expresses pure and serene gain and loss in his response: "Inferior
is then without-distinctions inferior." What I've rendered as "without distinctions," 總, could also be "totally," or "completely."

What could be more pure and serene than inferior just as totally,
completely inferior?

Good morning.

71

There is victory and defeat, no?

Yuantong asked: "The teaching sets up three vehicles. Still, there is superior and inferior too, no?"

Wansong replied: "Superior, in that case, is entirely superior."

Linquan's Verse

Superior in that case is entirely superior
How can it be intimately verified?
The Buddha ancestor steelyard
Determines the undetermined
Although not given to you on the same tray
Finally, the weight problem conceals the steelyard

Commentary

The three-vehicle teaching is common in the Mahayana. The three vehicles are those of the shravaka (hearer), seeking individual liberation; the pratyekabuddha (solitary sage), one who becomes enlightened through their own efforts and declines to teach; and the bodhisattva (awakening being), who resolves to awaken for the benefit of all.

Although the Buddha manifests these teachings according to the capacities of living beings, still, Yuantong wonders if there is high and low.

In *The Lotus Sutra*, "Chapter 2: Skillful Means," the Buddha says,

In all the buddha-lands in the ten directions
There is only the Dharma of one vehicle,
Not a second or a third,
Except what the buddhas teach by skillful means.
Merely using provisional expressions,
The Buddha has drawn living beings to himself,
In order to teach them
The wisdom of the Buddha.
Buddhas appear in this world
For this one reason alone,
The real reason.

The other two ways are not genuine.[158]

It sounds like there is only one genuine vehicle – the one-vehicle that contains as a skillful means all three vehicles, including what is usually thought of as superior – the bodhisattva vehicle.

Superior, in any case, is just superior through and through. But if superior meant best or better, then how could one's superiority be intimately verified? If you, for example, were the most superior practitioner, you'd be up there alone on the peak of wonder, after all. Who will provide the balance? To arrive at a fair measure, or any measure, for that matter, all the weight cannot be on the same tray.

Dogen in his "Expounding a Dream in a Dream," deals with this as well:

> Once we have obtained equilibrium, it does not hinge upon the object, the steelyard, or its workings. You must investigate the following thoroughly: Although hang[ing] in empty space, if you do not bring about equilibrium, fairness is not materialized. Just as itself hangs in emptiness, so does it accept things and lets them play freely in emptiness.[159]

In other words, the buddha ancestor steelyard determines the undetermined. Finally, the weight problem conceals the steelyard. The measuring device, our assessment of one and other, buddha and buddha, even, is obscured by the very act of measuring, although we're all hanging in empty space.

"The teaching sets up three vehicles. Still, there is superior and inferior too, no?"

---

158 *The Lotus Sutra: A Contemporary Translation of a Buddhist Classic*, trans., Gene Reeves (Somerville, MA: Wisdom, 2008), 88.

159 Eihei Dogen, "Expounding a Dream Within a Dream," in Hee Jin Kim, *Dogen on Meditation and Thinking: A Reflection on His View of Zen* (Albany, NY: State University of New York Press, 2007), 42.

72

There is shallow and deep, no?

Yuantong asked: "Nature and appearance are two schools, yet there are shallow and deep, no?"

Wansong replied: "Seeking the other, already impoverished."

Linquan's Verse

Seeking the other, the poor know it's used up
Completely interpenetrated, strong distinctions break up
A lord might incite someone in the same field to steal a
    small amount of money
Family discord! Deception in the neighboring village

Commentary

Nature, 性, and appearance, 相, refer to buddha nature and phenomena, the unconditioned and the conditioned, or essence and characteristics. Here, though, it is about the schools that approach practice from those two primary perspectives, particularly, the Huayan school that taught that all these arise from thusness, the dharmakaya, and the Madhyamika and Yogacara movements that emphasized dependent arising of phenomena.

One approach has got to be deeper than the other, no?

Similarly, Dogen was asked, "Because of what superior features in the practice you are now speaking about, do you solely recommend this and set aside those others?"

Dogen responded,

> Buddhist practitioners should know not to argue about the superiority or inferiority of teachings and should not discriminate between shallow or deep dharma, but should only know whether the practice is genuine or false. There are those who flowed into the buddha way drawn by grasses, flowers, mountains, or rivers.... I truly recommend practice which directly actualizes awakening, and am showing the wondrous way which is simply

transmitted by buddha ancestors.[160]

Or you might find someone who previously had nothing, but now has a lot of clever ideas about superior and inferior, deep and shallow, and ask them.

Linquan points out that as the world of this and that completely interpenetrates, 圓融, deep and shallow become like water and waves. Taking sides is like a lord exploiting their peasants for amusement, a family in discord, or conflict with neighbors.

When I was young, I had the chance to travel in Japan with Katagiri Roshi and visit many monasteries. After one such visit, where we had stayed for just a few days, we sat on the train and chatted. I shared some thoughts about what I saw as their rough style of practice. I was surprised, for instance, that after tea, the serving monks passed out ashtrays, the monks pulled packs of cigarettes from their kimono sleeves, and everyone lit up. And then there was the late-night, after-hours invite to sip home-made plum wine and smoke cigars in the kitchen, which I had enjoyed enormously. What had been a friendly conversation on the train suddenly ended. Roshi looked at me with burning intensity and said, "Do not speak about the practice at a place until you have been there for at least several months."

We sat for an hour or so in silence until our next stop. "Seeking the other, the poor know it's used up" indeed.

Friend, only concern yourself with the genuineness of your own practice.

---

160 Eihei Dogen, *Bendowa: Talk on Wholehearted Practice of the Way*, trans., Shohaku Okumura (Kyoto, Kyoto Soto Zen Center: 1993), 42.

73

How to treat the Four Maladies?

Yuantong asked: "Making, accepting, stopping, and annihilating.... How to treat the four maladies?"

Wansong replied: "The items on the right are equally divided."

Linquan's Verse

> The items on the right are equally divided
> Receive the handed-down precious teaching with feeling
> One pill cures the disease and brings calm
> Why borrow a donkey for transport
> When sun-face, moon-face respond
> Who's afraid of inquiring of the teacher through layer
> after layer?

Commentary

With this question, Yuantong again goes deeply into applying the teaching from the sutra tradition for liberation – a noble aim. So, let's meet him where he lives, within *The Sutra of Perfect Enlightenment*, "Chapter 10: Universal Enlightenment Bodhisattva." This chapter begins with Samantabhadra asking the Buddha what kind of person someone should seek if they are intent on going beyond their present experience.

Before unpacking the Four Maladies listed by Yuantong in his question, the Buddha first gives a few general criteria for a genuine teacher:

> Even while pointing out your various faults, they praise your practices of purity, and prevent you from breaking the precepts.... This Genuine Teacher constantly demonstrates purity throughout the four postures [sitting, standing, walking, and lying down]. Although [they] point out all kinds of errors and difficulties, [their] mind lacks pride.

The Buddha then says, "The subtle dharma that is actualized by this Genuine Teacher should be free from the Four Maladies."

These four are making, accepting, stopping, and annihilating. Let's look at each one.

For example, suppose someone who wants to achieve awakening says, "… based on my original mind I shall carry out various practices," they expose the symptom of the first malady – making. Because their attitude is to impute an original mind that is apart from them and apart from the practices that they employ to realize awakening, they are using the practices as a means to an end – a contrivance. Because awakening cannot be attained through manipulation, this is a malady of contrivance that must be abandoned.

Second, suppose someone says, "We should just naturally go along with the various natures of reality." Because in this there is a "we" and a "go along" it is not yet intimate and awakening cannot be attained when even the slightest separation is held, the accepting position is also a malady and must be abandoned.

Third, suppose someone says, "… From my present thought, I shall permanently stop all thoughts and thus apprehend the cessation and equanimity of all natures." Although absorbing oneself in stopping is a skillful means to calm the divided mind, it is a provisional achievement, subject to change, and not yet awakening. Thus, stopping is a malady and must be abandoned.

Fourth, suppose someone says, "I will now permanently annihilate all defilements. Body and mind are ultimately empty, lacking anything. How much more should all the false realms of the sense organs and their objects be permanently erased." Since awakening requires the arising of sense experience to realize true nature, annihilating all objects is an aggressive strategy that will also erase the possibility of awakening. Therefore, the strategy of annihilation is a malady and must be abandoned.

If all these strategies are maladies, how can they be treated? What is the cure for the disease of the subtly divided heart?

> When you are free from the Four Maladies you will be aware of purity. The making of this observation is called "correct insight." Any other insight is called "mistaken insight."[161]

Wansong says, "The items on the right are equally divided." In other words, the treatment is equal to the malady. I hope that brought a smile to your face. It's the one pill, referenced by Linquan in the verse, that resolves the great matter. No need to lug a U-Haul packed with texts as you move along your journey.

The verse reference to "Sun face, moon face" is a Mazu koan that

161 *The Sutra of Perfect Enlightenment (Yuanjue jing)*, trans., Charles Muller, http://www.acmuller.net/bud-canon/sutra_of_perfect_enlightenment.html#div-10

appears in *The Blue Cliff Record*, Case 3:

> Great master Ma was unwell. The hospital monk asked,
> "Venerable, how have you been feeling lately?" Master
> Ma said, "Sun Faced Buddha, Moon Faced Buddha."[162]

We take up the medicine of the dharma to exhaust it's potential, to exhaust
the medicine. Lingering in any strategy is a malady. Finally, we sit peaceful and luminous without manipulation. Each dharma, every buddha,
just as it is. Sun Faced, Moon Faced. Some last for long, some last only
for a moment. And yet when we make this newfound lived experience
into some *thing*, a malady surely appears. The dharma isn't a cognitive
reframe, *the* ultimate strategy that will save you, but rigorously letting go.
A thorough burning up and dropping off.

Actually embodying this is to receive the precious handed-down
teaching with feeling.

---

162 Yuanwu Keqin, *The Blue Cliff Record*, Case 3, trans., Dosho Port (unpublished).

74

What is the true moon?

Yuantong asked: "There is only one true moon. Changes during the night watch are neither the [true] moon, nor not the [true] moon. What is the true moon?"

Wansong replied: "Clear illumination where there is none."

Linquan's Verse

Clear illumination where there is none
Wonderous virtue turns the mysterious pivot
The cold of the golden wave is deep, profound
Stop, stop, the lonely jade hare
The crooked hook does not appear
The bright mirror slips – there is no head
As if understanding Yunyan's intention for raising the
   broom
You must know the fundamental without expending
   diligent practice

Commentary

With regard to the one clear true moon of awakening. Hakuin wrote,

> Followers of the Way, if engaging in genuine practice you bore through and smash open the dark cave of the eighth, or alaya, consciousness, at that moment the precious radiance of the Great Perfect Mirror Wisdom will suddenly shine forth. You will be astonished to discover that the light of the Great Perfect Mirror Wisdom is as dark as pitch-black lacquer. This is called the rank of "Biased within the True.[163]

Dark as pitch black lacquer. The first rank, the first taste of awakening.

---

163 Hakuin Zenji, *Complete Poison Blossoms from a Thicket of Thorn: The Zen Records of Hakuin Zenji*, trans., Norman Waddell (Berkeley, CA: Counterpoint, 2017), 418-419 (modified).

The bias of the this-and-that phenomenal world is swallowed whole by the universal, clear illumination of the true. This is the beginning of the process of awakening.

So Linquan says, "Wonderous virtue turns the mysterious pivot." "Wonderous virtue" is the title for the Bodhisattva of Wisdom, Manjusri, who swings the sword of nondual wisdom. The "mysterious pivot" is turning in the dark – the cold (aka, unaffected) – in the heart of the golden wave of profound, deep awakening.

The "lonely jade hare" in the verse refers to the rabbit that appears on the face of the moon, as seen through the lens of East Asian folklore. Said rabbit is thought to be the companion of the Moon Goddess Chang'e, and is depicted as incessantly pounding the elixir of life for her. So, at this point in the process, Stop! Stop! Give it all a break. Let go of all maladies! There is no hook, nothing to catch, nothing to get caught on, and no head in the mirror either – the last being a reference to Yajnadatta in *The Shurangama Sutra*.

It seems that Yajnadatta got up every morning and gazed at himself in the mirror. One morning, due to mirror technology in ancient times, where the mirror glass tended to disadhere from the backing and so go black, Yajnadatta looked in the mirror and saw no head. He ran wildly through the streets, screaming that he had no head. Rather than being mad and running through the streets, in this case, the story is flipped and Yajnadatta becomes an example of just gazing into the black mirror, the pitch-black lacquer.[164]

The seventh line of verse has a great deal of personal meaning for me. "As if understanding Yunyan's intention for raising the broom." The source for this reference is "Yunyan Sweeps the Ground," a koan from *The Record of Going Easy*, and the koan that Katagiri Roshi assigned during dharma transmission as our life koan.

It goes like this:

> When Yunyan swept the ground, Daowu said, "Very insignificant life." Yan said, "You should know there is someone who is not insignificant." Wu said, "What? There is a second moon?" Yan raised the broom and said, "How many moons is this?" Wu then stopped.[165]

Yunyan (780-841) and Daowu (769-835) were close dharma companions

---

164 *The Shurangama Sutra*, trans., Buddhist Text Translation Society, http://www.cttbusa.org/shurangama/shurangama15.asp

165 Wansong Xingxiu, *The Record of Going Easy*, Case 21: Yunyan Sweeps the Ground, trans., Dosho Port (unpublished).

and biological brothers They trained together for decades, first with Baizhang and then with Yaoshan. One day, sometime during their decades of being grunts in the trenches of monastic life, they are out sweeping the walks and had a dialogue that I'd paraphrase like this: "You really aren't amounting to much!" "Oh, yeah, how about the one who is?" "Right, there are two moons?" Raising a broom, "Which one is this?"

Linquan ends the verse with this: "You must know the fundamental without expending diligent practice." But wait! Isn't the fundamental realized through expending effort in diligent practice?

Give it up. Give it all up.

75
How to uphold this?

Yuantong asked: "Vimalakirti's expression of silence is not two. How do later generations uphold and share this?"

Wansong replied: "Thank the teacher for bluntly pointing it out."

Linquan's Verse

Thank the teacher for bluntly pointing it out
Both words fall apart
Now, who thinks that both add to one?
In this way, raise the song of the vehicle of the ancestors
Laughter extends through the East Village of the great
    realm

Commentary

The Blue Cliff Record and Wansong's *Record of Going Easy* make a koan of a passage in *The Holy Teaching of Vimalakirti Sutra*, Chapter 9: The Dharma Door of Nonduality:

> Vimalakirti asked Manjusri, "How does the Bodhisattva enter the dharma gate of not-two?" Manjusri said, "My idea is this: in all dharmas no words, no speech, no demonstration, no recognition; leaving all questions and answers. This is to enter the dharma gate of not-two." Manjusri then asked Vimalakirti, "We each spoke already. Gentle man, say, how does the Bodhisattva enter the dharma gate of not-two?"[166]

How does the bodhisattva enter the dharma door of nonduality? Between Vimalakirti's question and Manjusri's response, thirty-one other bodhisattvas respond. The koan version assumes that we know about all that and cuts it away. The sutra tells us that Vimalakirti also cut away all the words.

---

166 *The Holy Teaching of Vimalakirti: A Mahayana Scripture*, trans., Robert A. F. Thurman (University Park, PA, and London: Penn State University Press, 1977), 77. This, though, is quoted from Yuanwu Keqin, *The Blue Cliff Record*, Case 84, trans., Dosho Port (unpublished).

The koan version is so quiet that it doesn't even say that Vimalakirti shut up, but simply leaves us hanging with the question. "Gentle man, say, how does the Bodhisattva enter the dharma gate of not-two?"

Is the silence of Vimalakirti nondual? Is your silence nondual? As long as there is silence as opposed to words, of course, it is dual. Do you think that if you add up silence and words, you get the whole tamale?

What, then, is the silence of Vimalakirti?

Oh, if you explain it, you probably fall into words or body language, right? So how will you share the nondual truth? What is the truth that falls into neither words nor silence?

Wansong assures us that the teacher, perhaps Vimalakirti or maybe himself, has already bluntly pointed it out. How so? With words or silence? Both words, "words" and "silence," dissipate in the wind.

Linquan says that "In this way, raise the song of the vehicle of the ancestors." What is "In this way?"

Does the song of the ancestors rely on words or silence?

"Laughter extends through the East Village of the great realm."

A long-forecast snow storm rolled in this morning. I went out at sunrise to feel the strong winds from the south-east that have nearly wiped the sandy beach clean. With visibility limited, we'll stay in the Neyaashi Zen Hermitage today, venturing outside just to shovel the snow, and later to get a good look at the wild waves on the lake.

76

What is the source?

Yuantong asked: "For the Buddha's words, mind is the source. When the mind is not yet accomplished, what is the source?"

Wansong replied: "Where is there no source?"

Linquan's Verse

> Where is there no source?
> Each thing and everyone accords
> Fully actualized one *nen*
> Wonderful virtue is dignified and majestic
> Like Ever Wailing completely letting go
> You must know that stagnant water is not the dragon
>   storehouse

Commentary

One of the characteristics of Yuantong's many questions is his fluency with the words of the Buddha mind that form the basis for verifying awakening in the Zen school. He's already raised a couple of baker's dozens of sutras and at least as many koans. The accomplished words of the Buddha have the true mind as their source. What about the not-yet accomplished mind of a confused practitioner? What about this very mind?

Wansong's response is a question, "Where is there no source?"

Linquan claps along, "Each thing and everyone accords/Fully actualize one *nen.*"

As you may recall from "Question 7: What isn't pushed to change?" 念 is "nen" in Japanese and "nian" in Chinese. Meanings include thought, memory, remembering, moment, mindfulness, and study. It is the character that is often, perhaps too often, translated as "mindfulness" in English. The character itself is composed of the character for "now" (a roof, representing home) above and "heart/mind" below. I've suggested "nowfullness" as an alternative translation, but it has yet to wildly catch on. Even I, the proposer of "nowfullness", prefer to leave it untranslated because there is no English word that covers these many dimensions.

Fully actualizing one nen is dignified and majestic. For "wonderful virtue," Linquan uses the characters 妙德, here like in "Question 74:

What is the true moon?" This is the title for Manjusri, the Bodhisattva of Nondual Wisdom. And so, it is the activity of Manjusri that Linquan again calls to mind as dignified and majestic. These virtues, though, might not be what you think.

Linquan likens them to the Bodhisattva Ever Wailing, Sadaprarudita, "... the protector of the *Mahaprajnaparamita Sutra*. He wails in compassion for the misery of sentient beings."[167]

The verse ends with the admonition that stagnant water is not the storehouse or womb of dragons. How about the turbulent mind? Or just this mind? Is there some dragon lurking about in there in nowfullness?

---

167 *Digital Dictionary of Buddhism*, Charles Muller, http://www.buddhism-dict.net/ cgi-bin/xpr-ddb.pl?5e.xml+id(%27b5e38-557c-83e9-85a9%27)

77

How did you enter?

Yuantong asked: "No gate serves as the dharma gate. Yet say, how did you enter?"

Wansong replied: "Who is located outside the gate?"

Linquan's Verse

Who is located outside the gate?
Heaven and earth are not large
Perfect Enlightenment Monastery
long ago swept away the sutra
No need to carry a bamboo staff to knock down the
    moon
Breaking through the walls of the phantom city
nothing concealed or obstructed

Commentary

Yuantong may have had Wumen's *No Gate Barrier* in mind and perhaps this verse:

The great way has no gate
Among a thousand mistakes, a road
Pass through this barrier
And you walk alone in the universe[168]

How did you enter? The dragon howls, "Who is located outside the gate?" I'm reminded of this old case:

One day, the World-Honored One saw Manjusri outside the gate and immediately said, "Manjusri, Manjusri, why not come around and enter through the gate?" Manjusri said, "I don't see a single dharma outside the gate. Where are you coming from, telling me to enter through the gate?" On behalf of others, Xutang said, "I

---

168 Wumen Huikai, *The No Gate Barrier*, "Introductory Verse," trans., Dosho Port (unpublished).

202 ❖ *Dosho Port*

am greatly awakened."[169]

The phantom city was mentioned in "Question 67: Where is the treasure land?" It is a provisional resting place conjured by the Buddha in a past life to reassure weary pilgrims. Linquan insists on the collapse of the inside/outside paradigm. Anything else is taking a broom and running around in the dark, trying to knock down the moon.

Great and small, in and out, me and you – nothing concealed or obstructed.

169 Xutang Zihu, *The Record of Empty Hall: One Hundred Classic Koans,* "Case 1: The World-Honored One Breaks Through Inside and Outside," trans., Dosho Port (Boulder: Shambhala Publications, 2021), 22.

78

This is the working of what?

Yuantong asked: "To explain the one original movement of the mind is the working of the wild fox spirit. But when there is no original movement, this is the working of what?"

Wansong replied: "Still there is this red-bearded fox."

Linquan's Verse

Still there is this red-bearded fox
How miserable! An amulet in the armpit
The cognition of ordinary people is true presence
Karma is non-empty absence
Skillful as if clumsy
Wisdom as if stupid
How many children become people of excellent
    character?

Commentary

Explaining mind with mind, the shapeshifting ego consciousness can talk about the root source of delusion, just as enchanting as the wild fox who in East Asian folklore transmogrifies to become exactly what tempts you. Yuantong argues that if a practitioner realizes samadhi, this is the working of the fundamental itself, free from haggling with ego consciousness as ego consciousness.

Not so fast, says Wansong; this too is the red-bearded fox.

In "Question 47: What side of the matter?", Linquan raises the issue of the Wild Fox koan, quoting a line from Wumen's verse, "Two winners, one game." Let's review the portion of the case I quoted above and then go on to the full koan in order to touch what Wansong is pointing out here:

Every time master Baizhang spoke to the assembly, an old
man was there listening. When they left, he would too.
Then one day, he didn't leave. Baizhang asked, "Who is

this, standing here before me?" The old man said, "I am not human. In the past, in the time of Kashyapa Buddha, I lived on this mountain. Someone asked if even a great practitioner falls under the law of karma or not. Answering that such a person does not fall under the law of karma, I was born five hundred times as a wild fox. Please master, give a turning word and free me from the body of a fox. Does even a great practitioner fall under the law of karma or not?" Baizhang said, "Such a one does not obscure karma." With these words, the old man was greatly awakened. Making his bows he said, "I have shed the body of a fox. It can be found on the other side of the mountain. I would ask you master, please bury it as though a monk." Baizhang ordered the mallet struck and the assembly informed that after the meal there would be a funeral for a monk. In the assembly, there was much talk, as there was no one in the morgue and everyone was healthy. After they had eaten, Baizhang appeared and led the assembly to the other side of the mountain. Under a rock using his staff he dug out the body of a dead fox. Then according to ritual, it was cremated. That evening Baizhang came to the main hall and told the story. Huangbo asked, "That old man only gave one wrong turning word and was born as a wild fox five hundred times. Would a correct turning word have made a great difference?" Baizhang said, "Come here and I'll tell you." Huangbo went up and slapped him once. Baizhang clapped his hands and laughed, saying, "You got me! The Barbarian had a red beard, and here's a red bearded barbarian."[170]

Quite a story, eh? A dream in a dream in a dream. Ego consciousness talking about ego consciousness talking about ego consciousness. Just reading the case, you might find yourself so miserable that you reach for an amulet to put under your armpit or turn to Facebook to see how many likes your last post has received.[171]

---

170 Wumen Huikai, *The No Gate Barrier*, Case 2: Baizhang's Wild Fox," trans., Dosho Port (unpublished).

171 Such amulets were still popular in the time of Hakuin. Norman Waddell identifies them as "divine death-dealing amulets (datsumyo no shimpu; also life-destroying charms) Originally, Taoist charms were said to give the possessor life-destroying powers. Used like 'claws and fangs of the Dharma cave,' with which it is generally paired, in Hakuin's works. From Hakuin, *Beating the Cloth Drum*, trans., Norman

Anything to distract from the "me" of the past from the question of whether the self is free or not.

And this is it. Clumsy, stupid. The cognition of ordinary people is true presence, albeit unrealized. Karma is non-empty absence – this swirling in cause and effect is *mu* incarnate. Freedom is ongoing.

"Such a one does not obscure cause and effect."

Only a Wild Fox spirit would claim overwise.

Still there is this red-bearded fox.

Waddell (Boston: Shambhala, 2012), 216.

79

Where do the path and buddhadharma go beyond?

Yuantong asked: "Every saying of the buddhadharma is just words. Completely rinse the mouth for three days. Yet say, where does the buddhadharma go beyond?"

Wansong replied: "Just eat, vomit, spit."

Linquan's Verse

> Just eat, vomit, spit
> How many people see through?
> The Great Sutra
> No mo san man da
> San man da
> Words fill the whole world, a mouthless going beyond

Commentary

"Buddhadharma," "Buddha," as well as "zazen," and "kensho" are all just words. Yuck! Rinse out my ears, wash out my mouth! What's the real thing?

Eat, vomit, spit!

What?

Our Zen Way is the way of eat, vomit, spit, and all the broken bits and pieces. We turn toward what is usually thrown away, ignored, and split off. Our robes were originally made from the clothes used to wrap corpses and those used for menstrual blood. And in our work, we devote ourselves to the places that are usually not cleaned, like under the hedge:

> Once when Dainin-san was training under the guidance of Daicho Roshi they were cleaning the grounds at Taizoin. Daicho Roshi noticed that Dainin-san was not raking under the hedge. He scolded the young monk, "What are you doing? Look at the leaves under the hedge!" "Nobody cleans under the hedge," Dainin-san said. "Nobody cleans under the hedge," said

Daicho Roshi. "That's why a Zen monk cleans under the hedge.[172]

And in working with a koan keyword, in the place we cannot sweep, we do our utmost to sweep, just like Rujing instructed:

> The one word *mu* – an iron broom. Sweeping, delusion swirls around. Swirling delusions around, sweeping. Turning, sweeping, turning. In the place you cannot sweep, do your utmost to sweep. Day and night, backbone straight, continuously without stopping. Bold and powerful, do not let up. Suddenly, sweeping breaks open the great empty sky. Ten thousand distinctions, a thousand differences are exhausted with thoroughgoing opening.[173]

Sweeping with his utmost, cleaning under the hedge, and rinsing out his mouth, Yuantong refers to this from *The No Gate Barrier*: Damei asked Mazu, 'What is buddha?' Ancestor said, 'This mind is buddha.'" And Wumen's comment:

> Know that saying the single word 'buddha,' you should rinse out your mouth for three days. If you are a true person, hearing "This is buddha," you'll cover your ears and run.[174]

In the verse, Linquan invokes the Great Sutra, and quotes a line from the "Shosai Myo Kichijo Dharani," ("The Wondrous and Auspicious Dharani for Avoiding Calamities"). A dharani is an untranslatable sounding that invokes a certain buddha reality – here the wondrous method of avoiding calamities. The Chinese translators tried to convey the sounds of the Sanskrit by selecting Chinese characters that were associated with the sounds, and only secondarily, the meaning.

In Chinese, the first line of this dharani is "Namu san man duo." In Japanese, the line reads, "No mo san man da." "Namu" or "No mo," 曩謨, is the transliteration of the Sanskrit for "taking refuge." "San man duo" or "san man da," 三滿哆, transliterates a word or words in Sanskrit.

---

172 Dosho Port, *Keep Me in Your Heart A While: The Haunting Zen of Dainin Katagiri* (Sommerville: Wisdom Publications, 2019), 47.

173 Trans., Dosho Port (unpublished).

174 Wumen Huikai, *The No Gate Barrier*, Case 30: This Mind This Buddha, trans., Dosho Port (unpublished).

The characters mean "universal," but without referencing the Sanskrit original, that could be coincidence. However, since Linquan repeats, "san man da," universal, and it isn't repeated in the dharani, it seems that Linquan is invoking it's meaning.

Just this buddha great sutra, the universal prayer in which we take refuge. When words fill the universe, it is so quiet, and just this mouthless buddha goes beyond.

How does the "buddhadharma" go beyond? How do we avoid calamities?

Just eat, vomit, spit.

80
Disclosing Zen insight

Yuantong asked: "The founding teacher's separate transmission outside the teaching – to test, I invite this Zen person to disclose their insight."

Wansong replied, "A great flower blossom net."

Linquan's Verse

A great flower blossom net
Not willing to completely approve
Standing in the snow, holding up a flower
In the past they had barely met
Still he didn't spare his eyebrows and announced the
    noble wisdom
Warm weather turns cold, trembling, warm yourself
    facing the fire

Commentary

Yuantong begins this question with a reference to a famous verse by our founding teacher, Bodhidharma:

Separate transmission outside teaching
Not established words texts
Point directly human heart
See nature realize buddha[175]

Another translation has it like this:

A special transmission outside the scriptures
Not founded upon words and letters;
By pointing directly to [one's] mind
It lets one see into [one's own true] nature and [thus]
    attain Buddhahood.[176]

---

175 Trans., Dosho Port (unpublished).

176 Dumoulin, Heinrich, *Zen Buddhism: A History. Volume 1: India and China*, (Bloomington, IN: World Wisdom Books. 2005), 85.

The first documented occurrence of this verse was by Shexian Guisheng (n.d.), a late-tenth/early-eleventh century master in the Linji line, who attributed it to Bodhidharma. Our Zen Way is not established on words or texts, even those words or texts that say our Way is not established on words or texts. Indeed, the source for the stories we tell are finally unknowable and essentially unreliable. What is reliable?

Before addressing Wansong's response, a word or two about the translation of Bodhidharma's verse. Each of the four lines of the verse has just four characters, so it has a symmetrical visual presentation:

教外別傳
不立文字
直指人心
見性成佛

You'll see above that I've rendered it this way as well – four lines with four words each, so sixteen words in total – although, in English the symmetry doesn't work as well.

The translator in the second version used thirty-one English words. Whenever a translation is almost twice as long as the original, the translator is very likely adding meaning, doing the reader's work for them, by saying what the translator thinks the original says rather than letting the original speak.

With translation, though, there is always interpretation, and it is impossible to succeed. Specifically, in this case, the second translation makes the verse prescriptive – *by* pointing at the mind we see our true nature and *thus* attain buddhahood. It makes sense, but those elements are added.

The verse can also be interpreted in other ways, including as descriptive: "Direct pointing human heart." From this perspective, the human heart is already directly pointing. Always. Likewise, "See nature realize buddha" can also be seen as descriptive. When we see the essential truth, aka true nature (kensho), we realize buddha. We *do* the awake buddha thing. And when we do the buddha thing, we are awake.

In this context, Yuantong boldly asks Wansong to show him the nature that he has seen and is now seeing. "A great flower blossom net," reports Wansong. Such a beautiful image to embody in zazen. And in diligent zazen-samadhi within movement.

The characters that Wansong uses for "great," 摩訶, transliterate the Sanskrit, "Maha," like in Mahayana, the Great Vehicle, instead of the more common Chinese "great," 大. In this spirit, "This mind itself is buddha" is a Maha flower blossom net, like the net of Indra that extends throughout the multiverse, with a multifaceted jewel at each vertex.

And look! In this net of jewels is a luminous self, a word, an idea, a whole text – quite a bouquet of flower blossoms!

What about Linquan's verse? Well, to appreciate that more fully, you may need some more context. As you may know, as the story goes, at an advanced age, the great Indian sage, Bodhidharma, came to China and managed to get an interview with the emperor. However, the interview went badly, especially when he failed to know who he was, so he went north, and then sat facing a wall at Shaolin for nine years. Huike, a desperado waiting for a train, applied to study with the great sage by standing in the snow. He finally cut off his arm to demonstrate his sincerity. In other words, "Standing in the snow, holding up a flower."

The Buddha held up a flower on Vulture Peak and Mahakasyapa smiled. But here we have Huike's bloody arm held up. When we wholeheartedly enter the Way, we often find that we have to give up something of great value. It might seem like an arm or a fixed idea of who we are, but it turns out to be a flower blossom.

In the ancient Soto tradition in Japan, on the evening of December 9, following the seven-day Rohatsu sesshin, Huike's picture is put on the altar, as this is the day that it is believed that Huike cut off his arm. Then the monks again sit all through the night. On the morning of December 10, sutras are recited to requite Huike's compassionate blessings, such that what Huike had given up is honored still.

And although Bodhidharma (and by extension, Wansong) and all the ancestors, held nothing back in expressing the noble wisdom, even eyebrows or arms, Bodhidharma and Huike had barely gotten acquainted, so the old barbarian did not approve.

Standing all night in waist deep snow and cutting off an arm, after all, is not necessarily seeing nature, doing buddha. So

> don't wait for the person standing in the snow
> to cut off their arm help them now
> – Ikkyu[177]

Here, the weather outside is so cold that an arm might drop off even without the knife, -14°F as I write. We awoke this morning to find the Superior Bay side of the Neyaashi Zen Hermitage had frozen and in our (short) walk along Lake Superior, even the water was moving slowly, mist rising off in the distance. A couple crows played in the breeze. And, oh dear, you are trembling. Best return to the fire and get some warmth.

---

177 *Crow with No Mouth: Ikkyu Fifteenth-century zen master*, trans., Stephen Berg (Port Townsend, WA: Copper Canyon Press: 1989), 32s,

81

How will you walk?

Yuantong asked: "A distressed man on Shitou's slippery road. On the edge of Blue Jade Creek, how will you walk?"

Wansong replied: "Grasp the walking staff and raise it up."

Linquan's Verse

Grasp the walking staff and raise it up
Walking slowly yet moving
Heavenly musicians within the palace
Atop Vairocana's head
Shitou's slippery road! No merit
Blue Jade Creek road is clear and precise! Cut off
    thinking

Commentary

Blue Jade Creek is right here. Yes, reader, right here – right here in what we're doing together. How can we navigate *this* path together?

What's that? It's slippery, you say.

Indeed.

So too in ancient times, long ago and far away, before the rise of sectarian identities in the dharma world, teachers would send students back and forth, and a key part of students' journeys, with or without prompting, was to travel around and experience Blue Jade Creek from many perspectives.

Yuantong references one such incident with his "A distressed man on Shitou's slippery road." The story is as follows:

> Yinfeng was taking leave of [Ma]zu. Zu said, "Where are you going?" "Shitou." Zu said, "The path to Shitou is slippery." "I'll carry a wooden pole on my shoulder in case I come across a theatrical stage." Then he went to Shitou, circumambulated his seat once, shook his ring staff, and asked, "What is the essential point?"

Shitou said, "The sky is blue. The sky is blue." Feng had no words, so he returned to Zu and told him what happened. "When he says 'The sky is blue, the sky is blue,' make a sighing sound." Feng returned to Shitou and again asked, "What is the essential point?" Shitou sighed twice. Feng again had no words, so he returned to Zu and told him what happened. Zu said, "Always told you that Shitou's path is slippery."[178]

Yinfeng came looking for a stage upon which he could strut his Zen stuff, but Shitou slipped away before he could get cute. Sigh. Certainly, the Zen way, the human way, is slippery.

Try following your breath, the mind goes a-slipping and a-sliding. When I first met Katagiri Roshi, he told me to follow the breath. After a couple years with lots of daily sitting and sesshin, I came to him with a wooden pole and announced that I was now able to stay with each breath. He said, "Zen is not following the breath."

I told you the Zen path is slippery!

Wansong, in his response to Linquan, said, "Grasp the walking staff and raise it up." He seems to have entered the above narrative. Yinfeng pounded his staff on the floor. Wansong raises his staff high.

Linquan is inching along the path, hearing a heavenly choir of angels singing "Hallelujah," even. It's all happening in broad daylight, up on Vairocana, the Great Sun Buddha's head, and is not a matter of discussion or merit.

Clear and precise, shut the heck up!

---

178 Trans., Dosho Port (unpublished).

82

What is the one dream vision?

Yuantong asked: "Enjoying the mountains, abiding in the center, leisurely sleeping and dreaming with no concerns. Yet say, what is the one dream vision?"

Wansong replied: "Talking while sound asleep."

Linquan's Verse

Talking while sound asleep
The nation is completely broken – you cannot depend
　　on it
Xiangyan was silent while wildly hanging by the mouth
Could I ask for some water for the tea?

Commentary

Yuantong's statement that leads into a question could also be rendered, "Enjoying the mountains, Abiding in the Center [Bodhisattva], leisurely sleeping and dreaming with no concerns…" "Abiding in the Center" is a bodhisattva who appears in *The Sutra of Immeasurable Light*. Understand it that way, if you wish.

In either case, Yuantong asks about deep rest, samadhi, sleeping like a log. In such a place, what is Wansong's one dream vision? And how about your own sleepy self?

Certainly, he's talking in his sleep.

Linquan brings up sweet baby Xiangyan (香嚴, "Flower Adornment"), hanging by a branch, so he cannot speak.

> Xiangyan said, "It is like a person up in a tree, hanging from a branch with their teeth. Their hands and feet cannot reach any branch. Below the tree is someone who asks about the meaning of Bodhidharma's coming from the West. If they do not answer, they violate the question. If they do answer they lose self, lose life. At that time, what would you do? Show me!"[179]

179　Wumen Huikai, *The No Gate Barrier*, Case 5: Xiangyan's Up a Tree, trans., Dosho Port (unpublished).

Xiangyan here shares his one dream vision and he even invites us all into the conundrum.

Early in our koan curriculum, we ask a question that resembles Xiangyan's question: "Someone comes to you in a dream and asks, 'What is the meaning of Bodhidharma's coming from the West?' If you do not answer, you neglect your duty. What will you say?"

And we save the more difficult predicament of Xiangyan for a bit later in the night.

Bodhidharma, dreams, duties, and the urgency of a response. What is the one dream vision?

Could I ask for some water for the tea, please?

83

Where is a suitable place for dwelling?

Yuantong asked: "Yunju is said to have been fond of Jushan. Yet say, where is a good place?"

Wansong replied: "Going Through the Mystery Peak"

Linquan's Verse

Going Through the Mystery Peak
Endowed by heaven, solitary, remote
Plan to wade across the stretch of road –
The whip will snap your shin
Great seclusion in the marketplace, small seclusion in the
    mountain
Accord with the transforming person, both ways are
    incomparable

Commentary

Yunju Daoying (d. 902) was a twelfth-generation master in China through Dongshan in the Shitou succession. His lineage continues today in the Japanese Soto tradition. He was fond of Jushan, or Abiding Mountain. Yuantong is playing around with words here, saying in effect, Yunju liked abiding on the mountain. Where is my place?

It takes two to play at that game, so Wansong points directly to it. The mountain of form under the crown of the head – Tongxuan Peak, or Going Through the Mystery Peak, the mountain where Yuantong's hermitage was located. This very person.

Linquan knows this solitary and remote endowment. Arrive within this journey. It won't always be pretty or easy. Sometimes holding back from the common exchange by clenching your teeth. Just be this non-abiding person, actualizing the incomparable coming together of this life, whether in hawking your wares in the market place or strolling along a great lake while living in seclusion.

"Incomparable," 無等, is from *The Heart Sutra*,

> Therefore, know the prajna paramita as the great
>   miraculous mantra,
> the great bright mantra,

the supreme mantra,
the incomparable mantra....

There are so many pieces to this one life. To accord with each incomparable bit is freedom within suffering, abiding dead-center as the mountain of this life. So, Katagiri Roshi often said to me, "You are you, anyway."

84

What about on this mountain?

Yuantong asked: "My teacher, with flowers falling outside for not less than ten years, what have you been doing on this mountain?"

Wansong replied: "For years, no merit."

Linquan's Verse

For years, no merit
Not sticking even to the path
Pointing east for west
Crying south pretending it's north
Just passing through like this, insignificant and destitute
To the true eye, it looked like expending a lot of effort

Commentary

Flowers raining from the heavens were once considered an auspicious sign of realization. In the *Vimalakirti Sutra*, for example, after Manjushri and Vimalakirti had a rousing dharma dialogue concluding with Vimalakirti announcing, "All things stand on the root which is baseless,"

> A certain goddess who lived in that house, having heard this teaching of the Dharma of the great heroic bodhi-sattvas, and being delighted, pleased, and overjoyed, manifested herself in a material body and showered the great spiritual heroes, the bodhisattvas, and the great disciples with heavenly flowers. When the flowers fell on the bodies of the bodhisattvas, they fell off on the floor, but when they fell on the bodies of the great disciples, they stuck to them and did not fall off.[180]

Because the disciples were attached to non-adornment, you see, they stuck. Yuantong praises his teacher's freedom and asks what he's been doing all these years as a teacher.

---

180 *The Holy Teaching of Vimalakirti: A Mahayana Sutra*, trans., Robert A. F. Thurman (University Park, PA, and London: The Pennsylvania State University Press, 1976), 58.

Wansong has had "For years, no merit." His no-merit-for-years shows through his expression here with no flowers. Just. No. Merit.

Here at the Neyaashi Zen Hermitage, this mountain looks more like a sandbar. Some days, before getting out of bed for a pre-zazen cup of very strong tea, I lay wondering, with the great monastic traditions dead or dying fast, for whom was all the eloquence of the last 2,500 years of luminous dharma expounded?

That it should end up like this, in the hands of a bunch of ingrates like us, well, is just damn sad. The true dharma eye, even, insignificant and destitute through and through.

Yet, still, there is this flickering light.

85

What is not understanding?

Yuantong asked: "Now this mountain monk entirely does not understand. Is what has been understood not understanding? Is not understanding not understanding?"[181]

Wansong replied: "The teacher also does not yet understand."

Linquan's Verse

> The teacher also does not yet understand
> Playing with gruel and rice energy
> The earth's axis mysteriously turns the sky disk
> Closely woven literary warp and military weft
> Great pure gems are unpolished and uncut!
> The most precious pearls have no holes

Commentary

Believe me, I really don't understand. How about you?

---

181 A reference to Shitou's "The Song of the Grass-Roof Hermitage," found in Hongzhi Zhengjue, *Cultivating the Empty Field: The Silent Illumination of Zen Master Hongzhi*, trans., Taigen Dan Leighton and Yi Wu (North Clarendon, VT: Tuttle Publishing, 2000), 72-73.

86

How is practice for you?

Yuantong asked: "Not knowing is difficult. Practice is just distressing. Yet say, how is practice for you?"

Wansong replied: "Ask a teacher of senior rank."

Linquan's Verse

Ask a teacher of senior rank
Not maintaining opposition or obedience
Stop inquiring about defeat, danger, success, and
    gathering
Do not speak of regretting fortune and misfortune!
The source of the Great Way's warp and weft is self-
    leveling
No need to imprint the Sovereign of Emptiness' seal on
    your ass

Commentary

Not knowing is difficult. So, we practice tolerance for the inconceivable, going through the horizontal and vertical, emptiness and form, and being leveled through it all. Difficult and distressing!

Wansong only seemingly sidesteps sharing how it is for him. How it is for him is referring to a senior. Linquan seems to offer a correction for his teacher, saying, don't abide in the poor-me narrative of your life – the rough or the smooth. Raise a tough question, get a tough response. Be your life, not as a spectator. The ups and downs are the self. The self is the Great Way.

Now don't go out and get a tattoo on your ass that says, "Buddha."

87

How is the dharma source thoroughly penetrated?

Yuantong asked: "After much reasoning and debate, I've not yet penetrated the dharma source. After all, how is the dharma source thoroughly penetrated?"

Wansong replied: "Pick up your sitting mat and turn it over."

Linquan's Verse

> Pick up your sitting mat and turn it over – disclosing the
>   great pivot
> How many people reach this subtlety?
> Thoroughly exhaust the dharma source with no basis
>   remaining
> Suddenly awaken clear emptiness, diminishing the
>   enclosure you carry

Commentary

After all this reasoning and debate, eighty-seven questions into it, our friend has not yet arrived at the source. Conceptually, of course, we know he's already there. How can it be verified?

Katagiri Roshi once ordered me to "Turn over a new leaf – now!"
And it worked.

Wansong tells his student, "Pick up your sitting mat (aka, zabuton) and turn it over."

The mysterious pivot is fully and completely exposed and it's been there all along, and not just under your ass. But few reach the point of doing it, although many think they are. And then there's another type who think they aren't.

Walking the beach this morning after the recent snow, I noticed how the sand and snow have mixed, so what we walk on is neither sand nor snow. I pointed this out to Tetsugan, and asked, "What are we walking on?"

Smiling, she strode along with even steps, walking through the enclosure of reasoning and debate.

And so, the Buddhas and Zen Ancestors offer "Thousands of words, myriad interpretations are only to free you from obstructions."182 And in our tradition of koan introspection, hundreds of koans with thousands of keywords praying that you will "Suddenly awaken clear emptiness, diminishing the enclosure you carry."

Yes, you.

---

182 Ibid.

88

What is it?

Yuantong asked: "Perfectly clear, no obscuration. Always fully aware. What is it?"

Wansong replied: "Demon eyeballs."

Linquan's Verse

I'm fond of each remarkable person's demon eyeballs
Exhaust right and wrong and there is no winning or
    losing
What is it like being free from one-pointed not-knowing?
Meanwhile, younger and older practitioners knot their
    eyebrows together

Commentary

What is it?

And don't you make that demon eyeball at me!

Each and everyone, fully complete, lacking nothing. Remarkable! To realize it, yup, let go of gaining and losing. Just for a change, shut the heck up.

And now, not just demon eyeballs, but those creases between the demon eyeballs.

Gads!

89

What's the distinction?

Yuantong asked: "'Buddha nature' and 'dharma nature' —
what's the distinction?"

Wansong replied: "Dividing a day in two in order to
haggle."

Linquan's Verse

> Dividing a day in two in order to haggle
> Compassionately raising it up
> Not begrudging his eyebrows
> How the mind road conceals the treasury
> At night, the moonlight in the water
> In the morning daylight, the shadow moves along the
>   corridor
> Jade Creek's place for instruction –
> Fond of subtle, subtle critical examination

Commentary

Jade Creek (玉溪, Yuxi), by the way, is Yuantong's first name. Many contemporary Zennists get stuck here in subtle, subtle distinctions, enamored with the luminous flow, the mind road obscuring the essential treasury. Wansong holds nothing back, even his eyebrows, in compassionately pointing it out to Yuantong. Buddha nature, dharma nature, po-tato, pot-ato. Six of one, half-dozen of the same.

In his *Universal Recommendations for Zazen*, Dogen compassionately says,

> Stop the working of the mind and consciousness. Stop measuring mindfulness, thinking, and observing. Do not plan to make a buddha. How does this thing sit or lie down?

And

> Moreover, turning the pivot [with a] snap of the fingers, a pole, a needle, or a mallet; demonstrating proof by

raising a whisk, a fist, a staff, or a shout – this is not done
by pondering distinctions and making divisions.

Then

The treasure storehouse will open the self and you will
enjoy it comfortably as you wish.[183]

However, subtle, subtle distinctions are the place where Jade Creek learns.
Turn that subtle distinction-making capacity around to "… the moon-
light in the water…, the shadow moves along the corridor." The Jade
Creek flows to the sea. Clouds move through the sky.

Wave after wave laps the beach of truth.

---

183 Eihei Dogen, *Fukanzazengi*, trans., Dosho Port (unpublished).

90

The long journey: how is it for you?

Yuantong asked: "On the long journey of practicing properly together, say, how is it for you?"

Wansong replied: "Return having what? eye."

Linquan's Verse

Return having what? eye
One sentence wraps it up
Perfectly clear, clearly luminous
An arrow passes through a red heap
Hearing sounds, seeing colors – complete suchness
Going with and going against returns the same, none are
   without

Commentary

"On the long journey of practicing properly together, say, how is it for you?"

Such a lovely, intimate question from the trenches. Linquan gives his answer in verse: "Hearing sounds, seeing colors – complete suchness."

A return to the senses. And we return to the "hearing sounds, seeing colors" theme that we touched in "Question 61: Are there no Bodhisattvas of Compassion who enter the gate of the inner pattern?", and "Question 62: What is thoroughly penetrating?" We will complete this thread in "Question 92: Why follow sounds and chase colors?"

"Returning" reminds me of when I was Katagiri Roshi's attendant. A young person traveled by bus from the eastern end of Canada to Minneapolis to ask about Zen. After she had her meeting with the old teacher, I saw her preparing to leave the center. "How'd it go?" I asked.

She said, "I asked him if his years of practicing Zen were worth it."

"Really?" I gasped, admiring the freshness of her beginner's mind. "And what did he say?"

She said, quoting Katagiri Roshi, "'Yes, to see the world nondualistically is worth it.'" And then she added, "That made me very happy."

Yuantong might not have been as happy with "Return having what? eye," but the message is the same, wrapping it all up in one little package that's very close at hand. But say, what is what? eye?

Like an arrow passing through the raw red flesh of lifedeath. In the end, going and coming, hearing sounds and seeing colors is the body of thusness.

91

Why no enlightenment, no knowing?

Yuantong asked: "The virtues of nature are originally existent. Why no enlightenment, no knowing?"

Wansong replied: "Almost completely forgotten."

Linquan's Verse

> Almost completely forgotten
> How can they exchange toasts?
> Every square inch is spiritually luminous
> Joyful to accord with heaven's dignity
> Surrender, understand, and go
> A thousand mistakes, ten thousand mistakes
> Important, not mistaken
> Stop forcefully stretching a duck's neck and shrinking a
>   crane's leg

Commentary

"Virtues of nature" here 性德 (xing de) refers to "The possession by every sentient being of the qualities of [their] original nature, such as good/evil, delusion/awakening. The complement of 修德 – virtues attained through practice."[184] Yuantong, then, is juxtaposing the last question and this one, now asking, we are who we are, so why are enlightenment and knowing empty?

Seeing, hearing, smelling, tasting, touching, thinking – are all empty of own being. There is no seed in this avocado. So too with enlightenment and subtle knowing – empty, through and through. Wansong's practice is so thorough that he almost forgot – but what?

Even though it is "… joyful to accord with heaven's dignity," the way we are and enlightened knowing are so close that they can't even raise a glass to each other, clink glasses, and say, "To the buddhadharma!"

To realize this intimacy, Linquan offers a three-step Zen: "Surrender, understand, and go." And while you're at it, you will make "a thousand mistakes, ten thousand mistakes." The mistakes are important. The mistakes are not mistakes.

---

184 *The Digital Dictionary of Buddhism*, Thomas Muller, http://www.buddhism-dict. net/cgi-bin/xpr-ddb.pl?q=%E6%80%A7%E5%BE%B7.

A duck's neck is short, a crane's neck is long.
You are you, anyway.

92

Why follow sounds and chase colors?

Yuantong asked: "The root of afflictive emotions is empty. Why follow sounds and chase colors?"

Wansong replied: "Go through the method of a patched-robed practitioner."

Linquan's Verse

Go through the method of a patched-robed practitioner,
    the fruit is exceptional
The eyes and ears do not obstruct it, trust looking and
    listening
The bright moon above the blue-green limpid autumn
    waters
Many floating clouds obstruct daybreak beyond the dark
    mountain peaks
Within sounds and color; intoxicated, yet, sobering up
The six nations at peace, in this way, the source of the self
    is pacified

Commentary

Now with some sense of desperation to realize himself, Yuantong raises a long-standing theme in the Zen tradition that is clearly an issue for him too. It was raised in "Question 54: Which phrase is most wonderful?", in "Question 61: Are there no Bodhisattvas of Compassion who enter the gate of the inner pattern?", in "Question 62: What is thoroughly pene-trating?", and in "Question 90: The long journey: how is it for you?" These five chapters, including the current one, form a mini-course within the larger field of *Going Through the Mystery's One-Hundred Questions*.

So, let's riff with the Indian tradition, and the verse from *The Diamond Sutra*, Chapter 26, one more time:

Seeking me by using form
or seeking me by using the sound of my voice
A person walks a mistaken path

And cannot perceive the Tathagata[185]

Make no mistake – the Zen path is an iterative process and requires the spirit of repetition. The old dog, Shunryu Suzuki Roshi, said it like this:

> But we may find it not so interesting to cook the same thing over and over again every day. It is rather tedious, you may say. If you lose the spirit of repetition it will become quite difficult, but it will not be difficult if you are full of strength and vitality.[186]

The root of afflictions is indeed a tedious thing. We are free from the beginning, including within afflictions and chasing after sense experiences – sounds, colors, smells, tastes, touches, and thoughts. If we are already free, how can being one with the sounds and colors help?

Wansong responds, "Go through the method of a patched-robed practitioner." Stop debating and just go through the method! Get off of Facebook and onto your cushion! Take refuge in the method through the twenty-four hours.

The character that I've translated as "method," 方, could also be "leveling." So Wansong is also saying, "Going through the leveling of a patched-robed practitioner." As long as we stick up out of experience like a nail on our cedar decking and analyze, synthesize, and complain, we cannot realize the same, one mind of Buddha. Of course, it takes great faith to let go, to be leveled, and to realize that all along the deck and the nail were one.

Bright moon, many clouds, and mountain peaks all speaking with the Buddha's long, broad tongue.

---

185 *The Diamond Sutra*, Chapter 26, trans., Dosho Port (unpublished).

186 *Zen Mind, Beginner's Mind: Informal Talks on Zen Meditation and Practice* (Boulder: Shambhala Publications, 1970), 56.

93

What does a great icchantika rely on?

Yuantong asked: "A Buddhist monk dwells in reliance on four foundations of mindfulness.[187] What does a great icchantika dwell in reliance on?"

Wansong replied: "On the way to Interminable Hell."

Linquan's Verse

> On the way to Interminable Hell
> From the west, from the east
> Inexplicable happiness
> Receive and use it endlessly
> Not seeing the nobility of Devadatta before there are
>   words,
> Not like the music of the third dhyana heaven ending

Commentary

It really sucks to be an icchantika, an incorrigible who won't accept the law of cause and effect, who mocks the precepts, associates with lowlifes, scoffs at the buddhadharma, and ridicules the open-hearted way of the bodhisattva. Because an icchantika has no buddha nature, no potential for awakening, they are destined to spend eons in the Interminable Hell, the Avici Hell (無間地獄) where one is burned alive, dies, and is instantly reborn in fire, only to repeat this cycle endlessly. The ancient Buddhists had a vivid imagination when it came to describing the various hells. As for whether this or any hell could be a truly interminable thing, that is controversial, with some great dharma masters questioning if anyone is truly irredeemable.

So, in the Buddha Way there is the icchantika and then there is the Great Icchantika – a bodhisattva like Jizo, who renounces all the virtuous karma they've cultivated since time immemorial in order to go into hell to liberate hell beings. These are also known as icchantikas of Great Compassion. Our Zen tradition specifically honors the Way of the Great

---

187 Mindfulness of body, feeling, thinking, and dharma. Or alternately, observing the body as impure, observing perception as suffering, observing mind as impermanent, and observing that things are without a permanent and independent self.

Icchantika, one who goes beyond buddha, functioning freely in whatever circumstance they find themselves in. Keizan Zenji, for example, reported that "At twenty-five, emulating Kannon, I produced the universal wish of the Great Icchantika."[188]

And Torei Zenji referred to his old teacher, Hakuin Zenji, as the Icchantika:

> I first experienced distinct clarity on Lotus Blossom Mountain in the province of Omi, but when I later went to the cave of the Icchantika [Hakuin], I couldn't even open my mouth. Thenceforth I lowered my head from the clouds and sought instruction morning and evening.[189]

In addition, Master Kumu, for example, addressed the assembly saying,

> Someone has a child who does not have six sense organs and lacks seven consciousnesses. They are a Great Icchantika, a kind of not-buddha. When they meet a buddha they kill the buddha, and when they meet an ancestor they kill the ancestor. The heavens cannot contain this person. Hell does not have a gate to let them in. All of you! Do you know this person?[190]

I'm thinking that you do, in fact, know this person. Or you will find this person on the way to hell. Indeed, the first four lines of Linquan's verse sing the praises of this Great Icchantika of no separation:

> On the way to Interminable Hell
> From the west, from the east
> Inexplicable happiness
> Receive and use it endlessly.

Wonderful. And for you Dogen fans, I'd like to point out that in Linquan's "Receive and use it endlessly (受用無窮)," the "receive and use" is the same as in his Self Enjoyment (or Fulfilling) Samadhi (Jijuyu zammai,

---

188 Bernard Faure, *Visions of Power: Imagining Medieval Japanese Buddhism* (Princeton, NJ: Princeton University Press: 2020), 18.

189 Torei Enji, *The Undying Lamp of Zen*, trans., Thomas Cleary (Boston: Shambhala Publications, 2010), 74-75.

190 Eihei Dogen, *Treasury of the True Dharma Eye: Zen Master Dogen's Shobo Genzo*, "Going Beyond Buddha," trans., Kazuaki Tanahashi (Boston: Shambhala Publications, 2010), 318.

受用三昧).

Linquan then goes and brings up that anti-hero, the super evil Deva-datta, who out of jealously divided the sangha, and even attempted to murder the Shakyamuni. Incorrigible Icchantika! The Buddha of *The Lotus Sutra*, however, sees that even this nasty dude was actually a good friend:

> All because Devadatta was a good friend to me, I was able to become fully endowed with the six paramitas, pity, compassion, joy, and indifference, with the thirty-two features, the eighty characteristics, the purple-tinged golden color, the ten powers, the four kinds of fearless-ness, the four methods of winning people, the eighteen unshared properties, and the transcendental powers and the power of the Way. The fact that I have attained im-partial and correct enlightenment and can save living beings on a broad scale is all due to Devadatta who was a good friend."[191]

As for "Not seeing the nobility of Devadatta before there are words/Not like the music of the third dhyana heaven ending," well, there's no melan-choly when you're deep in one-pointed samadhi.

And if even Devadatta is a Great Icchantika, what does that say about your favorite villain? Or even yourself?

---

191 *The Lotus Sutra: A Contemporary Translation of a Buddhist Classic*, trans., Gene Reeves (Somerville, MA: Wisdom Publications, 2008), 249.

94

Great Vehicle and Small Vehicle conflict?

Yuantong asked: "There is conflict between the Great Vehicle and Small Vehicle, no?"

Wansong replied: "One has many kinds."

Linquan's Verse

One has many kinds
The peaks of mountain ranges powerfully rise up
Refined people soar high in the sky
Sumeru is frightened and ashamed
Some days, the blown hair [sword] is expedient
Slicing the diverse human world into accord

Commentary

Late in a sesshin with Shodo Harada Roshi, a wonderful Rinzai Zen teacher, we were in the midst of work practice. I was raking near the cabin where the Roshi was also raking. He motioned for me to come closer and he then gestured to the group of students working in different areas of the retreat center. In his strained English he said, "Some of the people are having such a good time they don't want to go home. Some are having such a bad time they can't wait to leave." Then he paused and smiled, concluding, "God doesn't seem to mind having many faces."

In the present case this issue is raised in terms of how many varieties of One are there? Yuantong asks about the Great Vehicle, Mahayana, and the Individual Vehicle, or Hinayana. That's his word, not mine. In our day, a Zen practitioner would be more likely to ask about the Soto and Rinzai schools, or just-sitting and koan introspection – there is conflict, no?

Wansong cuts through the bull – "One has many kinds" – while also showing his spirit of embracing diversity, quoting a Yunmen lineage ancestor Xuedou Chongxian (980-1052) verse that was picked up and developed by a Linji lineage ancestor, Yuanwu Keqin (1063-1135) in his classic, *The Blue Cliff Record*.[192]

Similarly, the great Soto reformer Menzan Zuiho (1683-1769) said,

---

192 Yuanwu Keqin, *The Blue Cliff Record*, trans., Thomas Cleary and J.C. Cleary (Boston: Shambhala Publications, 2005), 13.

"The Soto and Rinzai Schools are, without question, one track; there are no side roads."

People in ancient times like today, though, like to focus on the differences, what Linquan calls the peaks, and get all intoxicated about them. From the perspective of Mt. Sumeru, the huge, mythological mountain at the center of the world, all-embracing as this central axis is, is rather embarrassed by the pettiness of humans.

Linquan pulls out his blown-hair sword, and I remember my grandfather, Harry Andrews, a butcher for fifty years. Grandpa Harry sharpened his knives so sharp that he would hold the knife with the blade facing up and drop a sheet of paper on it. If the blade cut the paper in two, it was sharp enough for him.

Likewise, the blown-hair sword is so sharp it cuts a hair that drops across it in two, slicing the diverse human world into one. Yes, God has many faces.

95

True mind and false mind

Yuantong asked: "The true mind and the false mind are in accord with each other, no?"

Wansong replied: "In two, there are no two divisions."

Linquan's Verse

> In two, there are no two divisions
> Not daring to deceive each other
> Wondrous wisdom of thusness
> A pearl rolling in a bowl
> Only seems perfectly complete in one moment of
>   thought
> Stop seeking ten thousand beginnings and a thousand
>   endings

Commentary

Wansong's response here, "In two, there is no two division," is the line of Xuedou's verse for "Case 2: The Ultimate Path is Without Difficulty," in *The Blue Cliff Record* that follows the line that was his response to the last question, "One has many kinds."

> One has many kinds
> In two, there are no two divisions.[193]

Oneness that excludes two-ness is divided. The true mind that excludes the false mind is not at peace. Just don't be deceived and think that you're beyond deception. This is the wondrous wisdom of fallibility.
    In the *Genjokoan*, Dogen says,

> When our body-mind is not yet fully permeated by the dharma, we feel that the dharma is already sufficient. If the dharma fills our body-mind, we feel that something

---

193 Yuanwu Keqin, *The Blue Cliff Record*, trans., Thomas Cleary and J.C. Cleary (Boston: Shambhala Publications, 2005), 13.

is missing.[194]

So, relax your shoulders and allow your soft-belly to be soft. There's nothing more to get here. Other than being a pearl rolling in a bowl.

---

194 Eihei Dogen, *Flowers in Emptiness: Selections from Dogen's Shobogenzo*, trans., Hee Jin Kim (The Edwin Mellen Press, Lewiston, NY: 1985), 53.

96

How to investigate
the three subtle and six coarse aspects?

Yuantong asked: "How to investigate the three subtle and six coarse aspects?"

Wansong replied: "Don't drag along the morning dew."

Linquan's Verse

Don't drag along the morning dew
"Karmic action, movement, appearance" and so forth, are
    wholly allocated
As for the meaning of "devising names" – I'll leave the
    explanation for another day
For the time being, accord with the activities of living in
    the Zen grove

Commentary

Yuantong's question is based on a classification of the buddhadharma in *The Treatise on Awakening Mahayana Faith* – a text that had a profound impact on our Zen school. Katagiri Roshi walked us through it step-by-step, along with elaborate handwritten flowcharts that I still treasure today. And Tetsugan Sensei and I are in the midst of the same study of with our Vine of Obstacle Zen students as I write.

The three subtle aspects of mind are activity, changing, manifesting. These are explained in *The Treatise* in detail as follows:

> The first is the characteristic of the <u>karmic action</u> of ig-
> norance. The mind moves because of non-awakening,
> and this is termed "karmic action." When awakened, it
> does not move. When it does move, there is suffering
> because effect is not separate from cause. The second is
> the characteristic of the perceiver. There is a perceiver
> because of <u>movement</u> [in the mind]. When it does not
> move, there is no perceiving. The third is the character-
> istic of perceptual fields. Perceptual fields falsely appear

because of the perceiver. When apart from perceiving, there are no perceptual fields.[195]

The six coarse aspects are cognition, continuous flow, attachment and grasping, <u>devising names</u> (singled out in the verse), karmic action, and suffering.

Yuantong's question is about investigating the nonawakening in order to realize awakening. Wansong's response, "Don't drag along the morning dew," hides a subtle but turning point. The awakened mind and the nonawakened mind, you see, are as close as water is to waves and wind.

So Wansong's response is admonishing Yuantong not to investigate his experience as if he was outside of it! This is to wash mud with mud. "Don't you be dragging the morning dew into my house!"

Within the context of the Zen training container, the Zen grove (or "harmonious thicket"), the purpose of studying a text like The Treatise is to become one with the teaching – in this case, the three subtle and six coarse aspects - not to pretend that we're like drones buzzing above the landscape of this one great life. Such buzzing is just the wandering of the divided mind masquerading as practice. Indeed, we've been soaked through with sweet dew from the beginning.

Likewise, Linquan's defers analytic comment and directs Yuantong (and anyone really listening) into the vivid, living truth. Awakening is only found when we hide ourselves in the awesome presence of the active Buddha and immediately and directly take wholehearted refuge in the methods offered to us by our teachers.

Awakening does not come when indulging in and remotely categorizing experience as if living in a moon palace.

---

195 *The Treatise on Awakening Mahayana Faith*, trans., John Jorgensen, Dan Lusthaus, John Makeham, and Mark Strange (New York: Oxford University Press, 2019), 80. Modified, inspired by the translation of A.G. Wonderwheel.

97

How do differences interpenetrate?

Yuantong asked: "How do a thousand differences and ten thousand distinctions interpenetrate?"

Wansong replied: "Unfold both hands."

Linquan's Verse

Unfold both hands
Completely lacking possessions
Four in the evening, three at night
The disciple succeeded in crossing over misfortune
Vital to know the cause of interpenetration
With each passing year, winter is colder and colder

Commentary

Yuantong asks here about the interpenetration of all the apparently distinct phenomena. How?

Wansong gives a counter-intuitive demonstration – unfold your hands. How could unfolding demonstrate how the one thousand, the ten thousand differences fold together?

Linquan offers a reference to an ancient story from the *Zhuangzi* to clarify:

> In the state of Song there was a monkey trainer who liked monkeys and raised a troop of them. He was able to understand the monkeys' thoughts, and the monkeys also understood his mind. He reduced his own family's food to satisfy the monkeys' wishes, but soon ran short and had to limit their food. Fearing the monkeys might not agree with him, he first lied to them, saying, "I'll give you chestnuts—three in the morning and four in the evening. Will that be enough?" The monkeys all rose up in fury. Then he said, "How about if I give you four chestnuts in the morning and three in the evening?" The monkeys all quieted down, pleased. When people entrap each other through the differences in their abilities, it's always like this. Sages use intelligence to encompass

ignorant people the way the monkey trainer used his wits to trap the monkeys. The terms and realities may be equivalent, yet they cause them to be glad or mad![196]

So, we're like the monkeys in this story? Hey, Linquan, who are you calling a monkey?!

Monkey, indeed. Every morning Tetsugan Sensei and I wander out to the beach of the great lake as close to sunrise as possible. This morning it was about zero degrees (-18°C) and the water on the lake was transitioning to ice. With each wave the world tinkled with the sound of ice against ice embraced by water. Blue through and through.

That old cold dude Linquan ends his verse with this: "With each passing year, winter is colder and colder."

What is the cause of interpenetration?

When my armpit itches, I scratch it.

196 From "Book of Master Lie," from Thomas Cleary, *One Hundred Questions: A Chan Buddhist Classic*, Kindle Edition, 106-107.

98

What do you see?

Yuantong raised one finger and said: "Like Venerable Juzhi, right here, emitting radiant light, turning the great wheel of dharma. Yet, what do you see?"

Wansong replied: "Blind."

Linquan's Verse

Blind – who would have imagined, is double bright
A sutra of minutest subtlety takes a lifetime to complete
The fingertip was used by the child
Needing a genuine teacher, how many days' journey?

Commentary

Raising one finger and Juzhi have a rich backstory. Here it is in brief: One day toward evening a nun named True World appeared at Jinhua Juzhi's (810-80) hut. Without taking off her sedge hat, True World walked around him three times and then stood before him, saying, "If you can say an appropriate word, I will take off my hat." True World did not observe the proper ritual and Juzhi was unable to respond. This was repeated twice more, and then True World walked out.

Juzhi was about to leave his hermitage and search for a true teacher when a true teacher, Hangzhou Tianlong (770–850), showed up at his door. Juzhi poured out his practice issues and his trouble with women. Tianlong raised one finger. Juzhi then greatly awakened.

> When Juzhi was asked a question, he only raised one finger. Later there was a boy who when asked what the master taught, also raised a finger. Juzhi heard about this, and with a knife cut off the boy's finger. The boy howled in pain and wept, running away. Juzhi called after him, and the boy turned his head. Juzhi raised a finger. At that, the boy suddenly was awakened. When Juzhi was about to die, he spoke to the assembly and said, "I obtained this one finger zen from Tianlong. All my life I have used it, and never exhausted it." Finished

speaking, he passed away.[197]

Yuantong raised the story about Juzhi, raised a finger (presumably), and then pronounced that Juzhi's raising one finger emitted radiant light and turned the dharma wheel. He then asked Wansong if he saw this radiant light.

"Radiant light" (光明) is pronounced "komyo" in Japanese, is discussed in both the Pali Canon and in Mahayana sutras. In addition, it is the title of both a *Shobogenzo* fascicle by Dogen and the only known original writing of the second-generation Soto teacher in Japan, Koun Ejo (孤雲懷奘, Solitary Cloud Strong Heart, 1198-1280), *The Treasury of Radiant Light Samadhi* (光明藏三昧).

There are various types of radiant light, but here in *Going Through the Mystery's One Hundred Questions* as well as in the Dogen and Koun Ejo texts, the issue is whether the radiant light that humans can see that is emitted by the sun, moon, and stars is the same or different from the radiant light that is seen and emitted by Buddhas and Bodhisattvas. Or as Yuantong succinctly puts it, "What do you see?"

What takes Dogen 2,300 words and Koun Ejo 4,800 words, Wansong covers beautifully in one – "Blind."

This blindness is double bright in its utter darkness. For more on this see "74: What is the true moon?".

And much like Juzhi and the child before awakening, Yuantong is nearing the end of his one hundred questions and does not see the luminous teacher right before him.

---

197 Wumen Huikai, *The No Gate Barrier*, Case 1: Juzhi Raises a Finger, trans., Dosho Port (unpublished).

99

What is a peaceful person?

Yuantong asked: "For cooking, a frying pan with a cracked bottom. For sustaining the mind, gruel. Sitting peacefully inside Tongxuan temple, unconcerned about events outside the mountain. Yet, say, what is a peaceful person?"

Wansong replied: "A person who gets undeserved rewards."

Linquan's Verse

A person who gets undeserved rewards
A cloud keeps the moon company
When hungry, eat; when thirsty, drink; when tired, sleep
When like this, no need for idle praise and admiration

Commentary

Yuantong continues the comparison between himself and Juzhi, imagining himself in a mountain hermitage with a broken frying pan and a simple bowl of gruel as the whole world. As if to say, "I ain't worried about any nun coming in here and disrespecting me!"

But, hey, what is peace?

"A person who gets undeserved rewards."

American Zen priest Issan Dorsey said, "Everybody gets what they deserve, whether they deserve it or not."[198]

Mary Gauthier sings,

Yeah, we all could use a little mercy now
I know we don't deserve it, but we need it anyhow
We hang in the balance dangle 'tween hell and hallowed
    ground
And every single one of us could use some mercy now[199]

---

198 Michael Wenger, *American Zen Koans*, https://www.dragonsleap.com/american-zen-koans/everybody-gets-what-they-deserve

199 Mary Gauthier, "Mercy Now," 2005.

Linquan describes a peaceful life without praise or admiration.

I watched a bit of *Meet the Press* today and could only rub my head and scowl.

100

What blocks the cloudless sky on a peaceful day?

Yuantong asked: "Not seeking the bliss of liberation. What virtue would there be for the crown prince to wander around seeking a pearl?"

Wansong replied: "Misfortune comes in through the ego door."

Linquan's Verse

> Misfortune comes in through the ego door – surely
>   unexpectedly
> There are none who bore through thorough study
> with presumptuous deluded consciousness
> Baiyun crossed the valley, then leisurely relaxed
> What blocks being together with the cloudless sky on a
>   peaceful day?

Commentary

Yuantong's not seeking is not met with a warm and fuzzy hug. Like Wansong, the Grateful Dead sang,

> Well, the first days are the hardest days, don't you worry
>   any more
> 'Cause when life looks like easy street, there is danger at
>   your door
> Think this through with me, let me know your mind
> Woah-oh, what I want to know is, are you kind?[200]

Yeow! Presumptuous deluded consciousness just won't do!

What will do? My koan teacher, James Myoun Ford Roshi, met my first teacher, Katagiri Roshi, just after James had received zazen instruction for the first time in the late 60's at the San Francisco Zen Center. James says,

---

200 The Grateful Dead, "Uncle John's Band," 1970.

I was ushered into an interview with a senior priest. Dainin Katagiri Roshi, then called by the title sensei, was on duty. I made the bows as I was instructed and sat awkwardly before him. He asked how long I'd been sitting. I estimated three, maybe five minutes. He said, "Good. Keep that in mind."[201]

Linquan, meanwhile, is still thinking about the cleverness of his last verse and the line "When hungry, eat; when thirsty, drink; when tired, sleep," a reference to Baiyun Shouduan (1025-72), 19th generation in China in the Yangqi line of the Linji succession who had these Great Four Vows:

> When I'm hungry, I eat;
> When it's cold, I put on more clothes;
> When I'm tired, I stretch out and sleep;
> When it gets warm, I like to find a cool breeze.[202]

Here he notes that "Baiyun crossed the valley, then leisurely relaxed." Do the work, then enjoy the fruits, he seems to be saying. And Yuantong has not done the work yet. So, he closes his one hundred verses to *Going Through the Mystery's One Hundred Questions* with a koan that tests us all. Do NOT take this as rhetorical!

Present your one clear life now:

> What blocks being together with the cloudless sky on a
> peaceful day?

201 James Ishmael Ford, *If You're Lucky, Your Heart Will Break: Field Notes from a Zen Life* (Somerville, MA: Wisdom Publications, 2012), 48.

202 Andy Ferguson, *Zen's Chinese Heritage: The Masters and Their Teachings* (Somerville, MA: Wisdom, 2000), 430.

Postscript

I WENT TO WORK on *Going Through the Mystery's One Hundred Questions* in 2016, and now the first dusting of autumn snow of 2022 lays on the roof and grounds of the Neyaashi Zen Hermitage near the shores of Gichi-Gami (Lake Superior). I'm also aware of how my big sister, Mary Jean Port, seemed to be in the prime of her life as I began this project, but how she soon thereafter developed cancer, and died this past week.

Mary Jean, a sensitive spirit and skilled poet, was a long-time inspiration for me. One of my earliest memories is looking up while the four-year-old Mary Jean laughed wildly, her flowing golden hair illumined in the morning sunlight. What can I do but simply express my gratitude for her here.

You may recall the dedication early on in *Going Through the Mystery's* forward material – this phrase from Ashvagosha's dedication for his *Awakening Mahayana Faith*, a text that profoundly influenced many generations of Zen practitioners (including yours truly):

> I wish to have living beings
> Eliminate doubts, abandon wrongly held views,
> And give rise to correct Mahayana faith,
> Leaving the buddha-lineage unbroken.

Mary Jean would appreciate that Ashvagosha's name could be rendered "Neighing Horses." The story goes that whenever Ashvagosha was near, all the horses in the neighborhood would neigh in delight. Yuantong's one hundred questions, Wansong's one hundred answers, and Linquan's one hundred verses all seem to me now just the neighing of horses.

Each of these great practitioners, you see, is so adept in their role – asking, answering, versifying – while romping wildly through the wide-ranging buddhadharma, calling to us through their supreme delight. I gaze up at their masterful Awakening-Way fluency, how they so adroitly demonstrate the one great truth of this life through koan, sutra, and tender longing of the heart, and am inspired at what is possible in this life.

At the same time, I wonder, for whom was all the luminous light of these great Zen ancestors radiated?

My prayer is that this text will be like the neighing of horses calling to you, noble sovereign, about the possibility of thoroughly awakening and continuing the bright life of Buddha.

CPSIA information can be obtained
at www.ICGtesting.com
Printed in the USA
BVHW072317080223
658191BV00024BA/733

9 781896 559889